THE IMPORTANCE OF SMALL DECISIONS

SIMPLICITY: DESIGN, TECHNOLOGY, BUSINESS, LIFE

John Maeda, Editor

THE IMPORTANCE OF SMALL DECISIONS

MICHAEL J. O'BRIEN, R. ALEXANDER BENTLEY,
AND WILLIAM A. BROCK

FOREWORD BY JOHN MAEDA

The MIT Press
Cambridge, Massachusetts
London, England

This book was set in Scala by Jen Jackowitz. Printed and bound in the United States of America.

Library of Congress Cataloging-in-Publication Data

Names: O'Brien, Michael J., author. | Bentley, R. Alexander, 1970- author. | Brock, William A., author.
Title: The importance of small decisions / Michael J. O'Brien, R. Alexander Bentley, and William A. Brock ; foreword by John Maeda.
Description: Cambridge, MA : MIT Press, [2019] | Series: Simplicity: Design, technology, business, life | Includes bibliographical references and index.
Identifiers: LCCN 2018033820 | ISBN 9780262039741 (hardcover : alk. paper)
Subjects: LCSH: Decision making--Psychological aspects. | Interpersonal relations. | Social evolution.
Classification: LCC BF448 .O27 2019 | DDC 153.8/3--dc23 LC record available at https://lccn.loc.gov/2018033820

10 9 8 7 6 5 4 3 2 1

CONTENTS

CONTENTS

CONTENTS

FOREWORD

John Maeda

It's easy to get comfortable with what you have achieved over time. So it's useful to step back and consider how your state of comfort came to be. Was it earned through your sheer hard work? Or was it given to you based upon intrinsic advantages that you unknowingly enjoy?

The former narrative is what you're likely to prefer to tell yourself and to tell others as well. You persevered and overcame all odds. And your comfort is the result of a series of decisions that led you to where you are today as an independent-minded thinker. After all, why else would this slim volume with its unassuming title catch your attention?

In the parlance of O'Brien, Bentley, and Brock's new map of social behavior, you are most assuredly in the "west" side of their map. You are the accumulation of what you have done on your own. And based upon the wisdom of your selecting this book, you're always seeking to make the best decisions from the latest available research.

But something's stirring within your independent-mindedness. As you mature, you're becoming painfully aware of how the world is not about the choices that are made by pure logic alone. Instead, you come to realize that we more commonly make decisions based upon what others are doing—which was the premise of an earlier book in the Simplicity series, *I'll Have What She's Having*, written by two of the present authors, O'Brien and Bentley, along with Mark Earls. Because the simplest choice you can make is to not choose at all, that is, to have someone else choose for you.

With each realization, you start to move around their map. And the deeper implications of our fully wired society start to come into focus. You begin to see that the many decisions that are being made around you are happening in pack-like behavior that, unwittingly, you've already implicitly joined based upon your behavior online.

However, the online world can also be rewarding if you can manage to leave your own bubble—especially if you're lucky enough to come into contact with the concept of the Privilege Walk. It's an exercise in making visible certain advantages that some have and some don't.

With millions of views online, "What Is Privilege?" is a visually striking activity where everyone starts at the same line and then takes one step forward or backward based upon a series of questions. For example, participants are given instructions like "If you were ever called names because of your race, class, or sexual orientation, take one step back," or "If your parents both went to college, take one step forward."

The Privilege Walk is especially relevant to O'Brien, Bentley, and Brock's map of social behavior because it reveals the embedded, and otherwise hidden, privileges in the more individualistic "west" part of their map. There are so many multigenerational advantages, or disadvantages, built into an individual's identity. This made me find another reading in their work, "I'll have what others like me have had in the past."

My role as head of design and inclusion at the world's largest fully distributed technology company has taken me to remote parts of the United States and Europe that psychologically embody all of the authors' map quadrants. And I've learned to bear less prejudice against any parts of the map that might be considered any less favorable than other parts. Can individuals ever break free from the ideas of the people around themselves? Or can individuals break free from the ideas embedded in the generations that came before themselves? I'd like to believe so. How? By starting from a conscious understanding of where they stand on the social behavior map and then making the small, important series of decisions that can move them to wherever they want to be—preferably as far north as possible if they're lucky enough to make it there. Good luck!

Most of us serve on at least one jury in our lifetime, and we would guess that most people actually look forward to the experience, perhaps influenced by any number of television shows that portray the courtroom as an exciting place, full of points and counterpoints, eloquent arguments, and lots of surprises. For those of us interested in decision-making and how it helps shape the human evolutionary landscape, courtrooms are like living laboratories. In fact, it would be difficult to find a better lab for cataloging the kinds of decisions that humans make, how they make them, the speed at which they make them, and the ramifications—both short and long term—of those decisions.

Perhaps no courtroom has ever given us a better lab than that of Los Angeles County Superior Court Judge Lance Ito between November 1994 and October 1995, when it was the (circus) stage for the trial of former NFL running back, announcer, actor, and pitchman O. J. Simpson, who was charged with murdering his former wife, Nicole Brown Simpson, and her friend Ron Goldman. They were found stabbed to death shortly after midnight on June 13, 1994, outside Nicole's condominium in the ritzy Brentwood section of Los Angeles. A few days later, the headline in the *Los Angeles Times* read, "Simpson Held after Wild Chase: He's Charged with Murder of Ex-Wife, Friend." After his arrest, decisions began to pile up. If you're Simpson, how do you decide whom to pick for your defense team? If you're district attorney Gil Garcetti, you have the same decision: which prosecutors do you pick to handle the case? Next decision: where in Los Angeles County to file the case. Garcetti had two choices: downtown Los Angeles or Santa Monica, which is adjacent to Brentwood. The choice of venue came down to where Garcetti thought he would have the best chance of winning the case. He decided on downtown Los Angeles, which in retrospect was a terrible decision because it meant that instead of a pool of affluent jurors who were Simpson's peers, Garcetti was putting his case into the hands of a vastly different jury pool.

Speaking of which, both sides had to decide which potential jurors were acceptable and which should be struck. Attorneys will tell you that prior to the vetting process—known by the quaint Anglo-Norman term *voir dire*—they have to make quick decisions on how to rank potential jurors in the pool, and they have to decide which questions to ask particular jurors, often depending on paralegals and professional "jury pickers" for their assessments of various individuals' body language. For their part, jurors start making their own decisions during voir dire: Is that attorney really asking my opinion about something, or is she patronizing me (or both)? Is that plaintiff's lawyer as big a jerk as he appears? Can I really side with the state against a guy I've always looked up to?

Once a jury has been selected, attorneys have even bigger decisions to make, including the order of witnesses, which pieces of evidence to enter and when, how to examine and cross-examine witnesses, how to prepare their client, and what to include in (and exclude from) closing arguments. The centerpieces of the O. J. Simpson trial were a pair of rare and expensive Bruno Magli shoes, DNA spatters, and the unforgettable gloves that Simpson couldn't quite get on. In the end, after months of testimony, the jury needed just four hours to decide Simpson was not guilty.

Court TV (now truTV) covered the trial, as did several other networks, offering live coverage of the decisions that were being

Source: Courtesy of AFP/Getty Images

made. Millions watched the daily telecast, with the only other day-time broadcast rivaling it in terms of viewers being the 1973 Senate Watergate hearings. The loss in national productivity because of workers watching the Simpson trial might have been as high as $40 billion. As Lili Anolik put it in a piece for *Vanity Fair*, "[T]hough nobody knew it at the time, out of that horrifying crime something new was born, or maybe 'spawned' is a better word: reality TV." And, of course, reality TV of 1995 was a mere shadow of what it has become today, not to mention the fact that we now can get "reality" through scads of other media.

In our own work, we approach decision-making from a perspective that views decisions and their outcomes, intended or otherwise, as key elements of the enormous stage upon which evolution plays out. No matter how small or innocuous a decision might seem—to introduce a Bruno Magli shoe as evidence or to put a potentially lying detective on the stand—we can almost never guess the effect it might have on what happens on that stage. As we home in on sections of the stage, we get better resolution. Events such as the O. J. Simpson trial fascinate us because they are at a scale that is not so small that we can't generalize or so large that we lose all detail. This scale allows us to track different kinds of decisions, made at different times and of different magnitude, and see what the results, both short- and long term, were.

As humans, we originally evolved in a world of few choices, and not so long ago, economists looked at behavior in terms of rationality, the notion being that agents (usually) act rationally in terms of their choices and markets follow suit. Not so today, where economists have begun to look at such things as emotion and even mood to track what gets played out on the stage. This is why jury consultants get paid the big bucks and why even investment firms are beginning to staff up on the social, nonfinancial side of the house. Any notion that humans tend to think long and hard about something and then come to a rational decision has gone out the window. With instant access to "news" and views, decision-making has become rushed—too many possibilities out there—and we tend to rely more and more on the internet to make decisions.

With a public that is already overloaded with information, not to mention an ever-increasing gap between individual experience and collective decision-making, what does the future hold? A level of reality TV that we haven't yet imagined? Maybe, but that's a dangerous rush to judgment, and it's one that plenty of marketers, not to mention social scientists, are falling prey to. Studies of human behavior that result from mining the kinds of big data that are available on the internet are novel, but is mass-scale online behavior all we need to understand how humans make decisions? We strongly argue "no"—that we need to put those data in proper context. To that end, several years ago we developed a "map" of social behavior that helps capture essential elements of human decision-making that should be of concern not only to marketers but to social and behavioral scientists. One axis of the map measures how well people are informed about the risks and benefits of their decisions, and the other measures the degree to which people make their decisions individually or socially.

The three of us—Alex, Mike, and Buz— published a rudimentary version of the map in *I'll Have What She's Having*, which appeared in the same series as this book, and then a long technical article, "Mapping Collective Behavior in the Big-Data Era," in *Behavioral and Brain Sciences*. The policy of that journal is to send an accepted paper out to two dozen or so outstanding researchers in the field for comment and to publish those commentaries immediately following the target article. Then, the authors of the target article have an opportunity to respond. The comments we received reflected an astonishing range of scholarly expertise on everything from philosophy, to the psychology of emotions, to game theory in economics, to data mining in finance, and more. The comments then led us to make the model more powerful in terms of predicting certain decision-making behaviors and demonstrating how seemingly small decisions join together to create larger-scale evolutionary events. As Alex Mesoudi, one of the responders to our *BBS* paper, put it, "I see their scheme as complementary to calls from myself and others . . . to restructure the social and behavioral sciences around an evolutionary framework. Evolutionary 'population thinking' concerns the exact problem that is addressed throughout the target article: how individual-level processes aggregate to form population-level patterns."

Mesoudi was right on both counts. The model *is* a valuable guide to what he and others have been looking at, which is how individual-level processes aggregate to form population-level patterns. That is at the heart of evolution. The *BBS* paper, however, was technical, and one thing we heard from literally dozens of people, including some responders, was, "We really like the map and want to use it, especially the lengthy discussions of where various behaviors are located and the patterns we need to look for in order to identify them, but we need some help." By this they meant help in terms of maneuvering through some of the math, which tends to be highly technical. Those responses led us to produce this book, which we view as a user-friendly approach to the map of decision-making that focuses not on equations but instead on real-world examples of different decision-making behaviors and the evolutionary processes that underlie them. In the end, our goal is to show that there is more to understanding human decision-making than mining data from social media. But having said that, we still wish we had had Twitter available back in 1995 during the Simpson trial to record the "decisions" that millions of people would have made over his innocence or guilt. Of course, those millions of decisions didn't count—only the pooled decisions of twelve jurors counted—but it would have been highly entertaining anyway.

We take this opportunity to once again thank Bob Prior, executive editor of the MIT Press, for his unflagging support of the project. We also thank John Maeda, editor of the Simplicity: Design, Technology, Business, Life series, for graciously accepting our book into his series. This is the third book that Mike and Alex have published with Bob and John—the others being *I'll Have What She's Having: Mapping Social Behavior* (2011) and *The Acceleration of Cultural Change: From Ancestors to Algorithms* (2017). We also thank Gloria O'Brien, Regina Gregory, and the MIT Press's Anne-Marie Bono, Deborah Cantor-Adams, and Mary Reilly for their excellent editorial advice along the way.

CULTURAL EVOLUTION:
SMALL CHANGES IN THE AGGREGATE

Archaeologists are notoriously eclectic in their interests, but perhaps the one that is at or near the top of everyone's list is why, some 10,000 years ago, particular human groups gave up a full-time hunting-and-gathering lifestyle and began to settle down in permanent villages and turn at least some of their attention to domesticating plants and animals. In fact, it would be difficult to find an archaeological topic that has created more debate over much of the last century. Archaeologists used to believe that the process began in just a few areas—maybe first in the Near East and then independently in parts of the Americas—and then diffused out from those hearth areas to other parts of the globe. It is now clear, however, that the process happened independently some ten to twelve times in widely separated regions such as East Asia, Southeast Asia, the Indus Valley, and west-central Africa, in addition to the Near East, Central Mexico, and several regions of South America.

Without question, the transition to settled life and plant and animal domestication led to dramatic changes in prehistoric lifestyles—prehistorian V. Gordon Childe went so far as to term it the "Neolithic Revolution"—but we still don't know a lot of the details about why and how it happened.

When Mike was an undergraduate at Rice University in the early 1970s, he was fortunate to have as his advisor Near Eastern archaeologist Frank Hole. Rice was known primarily for its engineering and hard sciences, and its social- and behavioral-science faculty was small. Mike didn't consciously "decide" to ask Frank to be his advisor because there was no decision to make: Frank was the only archaeologist on the faculty at the time. Not surprising, the number of archaeology students was small—one to be exact—and because that student needed an advisor, Frank didn't have the luxury of "deciding" which students to accept or to pass along to another faculty member. He was stuck with Mike.

Frank was an expert in early agricultural communities in western Iran, which had become a go-to region for examining the relationship between early village formation and the domestication of plants and animals some 10,000 years ago. Frank had received his PhD from the University of Chicago in 1961, working with Robert Braidwood on how the origins of agriculture related to the beginnings of permanent villages in western Iran. Braidwood—who, incidentally, was the inspiration for the Abner Ravenwood character in the Indiana Jones movies (Ravenwood had been Jones's advisor)—was already famous for his excavations at the Neolithic site of Jarmo in the Zagros Mountains of western Iran between 1948 and 1955. What made Braidwood's work innovative was his research team, which included not only archaeologists but also specialists in fields such as botany and zoology. After all, if you're interested in the origins of domestication, you have to not only identify the plant and animal remains but also determine whether they were being domesticated as opposed to being gathered wild.

Braidwood didn't like the proposals that had been made for why domestication arose, taking particular aim at Childe, whose "oasis theory" posited that humans, animals, and plants had been drawn to water holes during periods of climatic stress at the end of the Pleistocene, 11,700 years ago. Given their newfound "closeness," all three became domesticated as a group. Plants flourished and attracted animals, which tended to stay around because the plants were a reliable food source. Humans also were attracted to the plants, and the animals became used to their being there and eventually became domesticated. Braidwood nixed the oasis theory and

Source: Courtesy of Marcin Szymczak, Shutterstock

proposed as an alternative that early post-Pleistocene villages were located along the "hilly flanks" of the Zagros. Instead of emphasizing environmental degradation as a cause, as Childe had done, Braidwood viewed village formation and domestication as being parts of a "settling in" by Neolithic groups—a period during which they experimented with food storage, sickles, grinding stones, and other pieces of technology so that they were, as he put it, "ready" for agriculture. How did Braidwood explain the absence of food production prior to the "revolution"? He put it this way: "[C]ulture was not ready to achieve it."

CLASSIFYING CULTURES

As strange as that statement seems today—that culture has to be "ready" for something—Braidwood was operating under a well-known and widely accepted framework dating back to the late-nineteenth-century work of Edward B. Tylor, Lewis Henry Morgan, and other social scientists who saw all of humankind, irrespective of time or place, as having moved through a preordained series of cultural levels, beginning with savagery, then barbarism, and finally, for the lucky few who were "ready" for it, civilization. Variation among cultures existed because not all groups were capable of making it up the ladder. The "simple" societies known to nineteenth-century ethnographers were akin to prehistoric societies that had stalled at various points on their trip up the ladder of progress. Morgan used a battery of comparative data to pigeonhole various cultures into those three units and even created three subunits each for barbarism and savagery. He also laid out a series of characteristics that formed the basis for placing groups in one subunit or another.

Some characteristics were subsistence and technology based—what groups ate, how they prepared food, what kinds of weapons they used, and so on—but Morgan placed heavy reliance on marriage and family. For example, all societies began as "hordes living in promiscuity," with some groups advancing to brother–sister marriage, then (for some) to group marriage, then to paired males and females who lived with other people, then to husbands and multiple wives, and finally, for "civilized" groups, the move to monogamous pairs.

Not surprising, the cultures that Morgan saw as "progressing" to the level of civilization were those that had a lot to do with the rise of modern western nations—for example, Rome, Greece, and Egypt. Civilizations, of course, are based around cities, and in a highly influential paper titled "The Urban Revolution," which appeared in a 1950 issue of *Town Planning Review*, Childe added to Tylor and Morgan's scheme by listing ten key criteria for defining true cities, including the presence of monumental public buildings, conceptualized and sophisticated styles of art, writing, full-time craft specialization, and a ruling class.

We refer to schemes such as the ones proposed by Tylor, Morgan, and Childe as *orthogenetic*, meaning that the things that are evolving—here groups or cultures—have some innate tendency to evolve in a predetermined direction. Morgan went so far in his lengthy 1877 treatise, *Ancient Society*, to state that "the experience of mankind has run in nearly uniform channels; that human necessities in similar conditions have been substantially the same." This view came to be known in the social sciences, particularly anthropology, as the "psychic unity of mankind." Under such an evolutionary scheme, decision-making plays little or no role, certainly not at the aggregate level. Rather, things are what they are. Anthropologist

5

Eleanor Leacock pointed out as late as 1963 that, "the general sequence of stages has been written into our understanding of pre-history and interpretation of archaeological remains, as a glance at any introductory anthropology text will indicate."

INTENT AND OUTCOMES

The orthogenetic view of cultural evolution is still around in various guises, but by the 1960s even Braidwood and his contemporaries were focusing on people and their decision-making—hence, Braid-wood's admonition not to lose sight of the "Indian behind the arti-fact." Placing individual "agency" inside the notion of culture being "ready" for a big technological change reminds us of a skit from the British television show "That Mitchell and Webb Look," in which two guys from a region whose inhabitants live in the Bronze Age visit a pair of Neolithic ("Stone Age") men in a neighboring village to describe the benefits of bronze over stone. They declare, "Stone is dead; long live Bronze!" and present their Neolithic neighbors with a bronze plate, a bronze mug, and even bronze shoes. The argument that people were "ready" for culture applied equally to the origins of domestication: people sitting around a campfire and "deciding" they were ready to start living in permanent villages and to begin domes-ticating the barley, wheat, and legumes that grew around them as well as the sheep and goats that grazed on the plants.

There is, however, faulty reasoning at play here. As archaeologist Robert Bettinger and biologist Peter Richerson put it, cultural behav-iors practiced over many generations do not necessarily result from their "likely" motives in the moment. Yes, individual-level decisions aggregate to form population-level patterns, but this is no warrant for attributing behavioral patterns observed at the population level to *intent* and *motives* at the individual level. So much for sitting around the campfire and deciding whether your group "needs" to settle down—or is even "ready" for it. From an evolutionary point of view, all that really matters are the downstream consequences of the decisions that were made.

A DIFFERENT LOOK AT DOMESTICATION

It was into this tug-of-war between intent and outcome that botanist and archaeologist David Rindos entered with the publication of his 1984 book, *The Origins of Agriculture: An Evolutionary Perspective.* In it, Rindos argued that plant domestication was not an all-or-nothing proposition. Rather, there were distinct phases within a continuous human–plant interaction process, irrespective of geographical locale. Rindos set off a firestorm because, as some saw it, he had dehumanized people as pawns of nature. As he put it, although human intent and innovation/invention undoubtedly took place, agricultural origins can be explained without reference to them. In other words, domestication was a long process, in which human behaviors— decisions—evolved in concert with those of the plants. Why, Rindos asked, when there are so many examples in nature of nonhuman, mutualistic systems of domestication—ants and acacias, squirrels and oak trees, for example—do we afford human–plant agriculture a special place? Why should we view the relations that humans and plants have developed over thousands of years any differently than we do the mutualistic behaviors of other animals and their plants?

The take-home message should be clear: people make decisions all the time—they intend to do something—but the outcome may have little to do with the intent behind the decision. Who would doubt that a Neolithic food gatherer in ninth-millennium BC

Anatolia, when he dug a shallow hole and dropped in a barley seed, didn't intend to raise a plant? Similarly, who would doubt that when a fourth millennium BC food gatherer in the Tehuacán Valley of Highland Mexico dumped a clay-lined basket of water on his fledgling corn plants he wasn't trying to keep them alive? The point is that, as real as intentions are in the moment, and as important as they are in increasing variation in cultural systems, they play only proximal roles in cultural *evolution*. We have to be careful when we link intentions to evolutionary outcomes because at the *population level* intentions play decidedly lesser roles. People make choices, Rindos wrote, but as far as evolution is concerned, they cannot always direct the variation from which they choose. In other words, we choose from among available options, but the range of options has already been determined by evolutionary processes acting on previous generations of variants. Alexander Alland earlier made a similar argument: "[I]ndividuals do not have to know why a certain act is adaptive for it to be adaptive. They don't even have to know that they are performing certain repetitive acts for those acts to alter [their] survival capacity." It's almost like asking what went through the minds of individual jurors in the Simpson murder trial. It might be kind of fun to ask them how, when, and why they reached their personal decisions—and plenty of people make a lot of money doing exactly this after verdicts are read—but for us, all that really matters is that he was found not guilty.

SOCIAL INFLUENCE

So far, we have not yet discussed a major theme in this book: social influence. Individuals make decisions, but they can, and often are, influenced by those around them. Underlying the O. J. Simpson verdict, for example, was a lot of social influence. That's the way juries work. Jurors discuss the evidence, attempt to persuade others to adopt their point of view, and hence reach (or not) a collective decision. One report had it that as soon as the Simpson jury was tucked away to begin its deliberations, members took a straw vote, which showed a 10–2 majority for acquittal. It took only four hours to reach the final verdict, which meant that the two jurors not initially convinced of Simpson's innocence were quickly influenced to change their votes. Neolithic food gatherers did not move quite so rapidly in their transition to domestication, but the same process, social influence, undoubtedly played a strong role. As we will see throughout the book, the degree of social influence on decision-making is an empirical question—one that gains increasing importance in today's world, in which behavioral scientists, not to mention market researchers, rely increasingly on crowdsourcing as a means of determining how and why people decide to do the things they do.

Published in 2004, before social media were widespread, James Surowiecki's best seller, *The Wisdom of Crowds*, popularized the premise that if you ask a question of a group of diverse, independent people, the errors in their answers statistically cancel, yielding useful information. The archetypical example is asking a hundred people each to guess, by closed written ballot, the number of marbles in a large glass bowl. Take all the estimates, add them, and divide by a hundred, and the resulting average should be surprisingly close to the actual number of marbles. To get a better estimate, you recruit a thousand people to do the guessing instead of a hundred. If you look only at the title of Surowiecki's book, you'll be like most market researchers and want to "crowdsource" solutions to your problems. Maybe you'll post a ten-minute survey on the web and ask for detailed feedback on ordering a replacement bulb online or buying a tank of gas off of Interstate 40. Those who read his book closely, however, will note that Surowiecki emphasizes how the wisdom-of-crowds effect is lost if agents *are not thinking independently* and are being influenced by their neighbors' estimates.

We wonder what the agricultural revolution would have looked like if social media had existed in the Neolithic period. In a sense, social media did exist as people signaled their social identity through pottery designs and possibly clothing, tattoos, jewelry, and other stylistic distinctions. British archaeologist Stephen Shennan was among the first to show that designs from pottery in Neolithic Germany show patterns of herdlike drift over time. But, of course, none of this had the speed or global visibility of modern social media. If the first farmers of the Near East could have YouTubed their practices to Mesolithic Britain—Mesolithic meaning they were still hunter–gatherers—then the transition to settled village life and the domestication of plants and animals in Europe would have occurred more quickly. Neolithic people with social media could have followed their favorite leaders to see which behaviors were trending in real time. Instead of individual, independent decisions being made over countless generations and passed down from parent to child—which seeds to plant, which fields to clear, which seeds to store and which to eat—decisions could have been crowdsourced. Deep understanding of the land, climate, animals, and plants, which had served humankind well for tens of millennia, would have been swamped as people turned to quick fixes adopted by their neighbors.

As we will see in chapter 4, not everyone has to be an independent thinker, at least not all the time. Helpfully, humans can switch between being independent thinkers and socially mediated copiers. It might sound simple, but the balance between the two is important to how communities behave. This finding has been seen in fish schools, bird flocks, and animal herds, where experiments reveal, for example, that logical, coordinated behavior of an entire group can result from a majority of individuals that are copying their neighbors and a minority—less than 5 percent—that are acting independently, such as swimming toward a physical target. A school of fish might look as if all the individuals know where they are going, when, in fact, very few are so well informed but their swimming direction instantaneously diffuses through the school by means of rapid-fire social learning.

A FORMATIVE-PERIOD CALL TO ACTION

We would love to be able to go back in time and to view up close the processes that humans went through in the long transition to domestication. How often were independent decisions made, say, in Frank Hole's 10,000-year-old Neolithic village of Ali Kosh, located in the hills of the Zagros Mountains, versus how many socially mediated decisions? Of course, maybe we have it all wrong. Instead of a long transition, full of innovators and borrowers, maybe it was a whole lot simpler. Maybe someone made an executive decision that the group needed to change things up for the better. A bit like the Bronze-Age management sketch we introduced earlier, this is how archaeologist Don Lathrap lampooned Rindos's intent-free argument. Standing on an escarpment in the Tehuacán Valley of Mexico on December 31, 1501 BC—during what is known as the Early Formative period—the head of a small band is making his usual 4:40 p.m. announcements:

Hey guys, I figured it out. Calculating with my gambling sticks, it turns out that the corn in the little patch over in the barranca will now give us more calories per hectare than that old fashioned, obsolete, mesquite down on the flood plain. Only one progressive thing to do. Tomorrow we all got to get down there and grub out all of that nasty old wild mesquite, and put the whole flood plain in corn. Hey gals, you got a big day tomorrow too, got to invent that thin, hard, technologically sophisticated pottery that goes with the real Formative. We all got to put our minds to how you throw up a permanent house, otherwise we won't make the grade. Remember this is it, the Formative Revolution. Get with it: we're goin' to make history!

Like we said, maybe we have it all wrong. Maybe it's a whole lot less complicated than we suspect. Let's turn the page and settle on a few handy terms we'll need as we explore the issue.

2

GETTING OUR TERMS STRAIGHT

How culture evolves through decision-making is not a question of intended progress but rather one imbedded in the kind of evolution that Charles Darwin laid out in his 1859 treatise, *On the Origin of Species by Means of Natural Selection.* Darwin radicalized the manner in which evolution in the natural world was viewed, changing the perspective from one that focused on evolution as biological "progress" to one that viewed it as a process of change. In his 1809 work, *Philosophie Zoologique,* Jean-Baptiste Lamarck popularized the view of a directionality to natural variation, arguing that organisms simply acquire whatever they need to live. This "progressive" brand of evolution is akin to the "great chain of being" of Medieval Christianity and almost identical to the nineteenth-century cultural evolution of Edward B. Tylor and Lewis Henry Morgan. Although he never wrote about humans, we suspect Lamarck would have loved the idea that human decisions drive cultural evolution in their intended direction.

Darwin shifted attention away from individual organisms as primary units of focus and toward groups of biologically related individuals, or *species*. Under this view, species evolved, rather than the individuals within them. This obviously has significant bearing on our discussion of intent and consequence as they relate to decision-making. For Darwin, the evolutionary differences among species were attributable to "descent with modification," with *natural selection* being the chief agent of modification—hence its place of honor in the title of his 1859 book.

EVOLUTIONARY TERMS

Communicating evolution can be challenging because its core technical terms are also everyday words, particularly *selection, drift, adaptation*, and *fitness*. In particle physics, by contrast, strange-sounding terms—*quark, meson, lepton*—have specific, unique, and unchanging definitions. There is no possibility of confusing them with everyday words. We would never say, for example, "You get my muon, don't you?" or "I'm going to go work out at the neutrino center." People do, of course, use those common phrases with "drift" and "fitness." Even the words *evolution* and *evolve* are everywhere, from hair products to the title of an alternative music album by the Imagine Dragons. Even more confusing for understanding the process of evolution, *evolve* is often used to connote intentional, *personal* improvement, such as pithy advice for you to "evolve into a more loving consciousness." In short, evolution is conflated with *change*.

This is why we need to define evolutionary terms as we will use them here. We start with *evolution* itself, borrowing a definition from ethologist John Endler, who defines it as any net directional change or cumulative change in characteristics of organisms or groups of organisms over generations. Notice a subtlety here: evolution is change, but change is not necessarily evolution. Darwinian evolution requires that four specific conditions are met. First, variation exists among a set of organisms in terms of the traits they possess. Second, some of those traits are more advantageous to possess than others. Third, the variation is heritable, meaning that it can be passed from generation to generation. Fourth, there is a means of sorting among the variables, which weeds out certain individuals that possess less advantageous traits. That latter process is *selection*. In everyday language, selection implies an intentional choice among options. Unfortunately, this definition makes it sound as if selection makes decisions about which organisms make it and which ones don't. Darwin himself made it sound as if selection were the final arbiter between life and death, but that wasn't what he meant. Selection doesn't "select" anything; it is simply a process, the end result being that some lines of organisms make it and others do not.

Related terms are *adaptation* and its close cousin *adaptedness*, more often referred to as *fitness*. Evolutionary fitness is the state an organism is in as a result of its evolutionary history, or, to use Darwin's term, because of its "descent" from an ancestor, and from that ancestor's ancestor, and so on. Adaptation is a bit trickier because it refers to both a *process* through which members of a population become suited over generations to survive and reproduce—that is, they become more "fit"—and a particular *feature* of an organism or of a set of organisms that has come about by natural selection because it serves a particular function and thus increases the fitness of its carriers.

Selection and adaptation are not the only processes involved in evolution. One other, often misunderstood process is *drift*, which is the random component in evolution. It is most noticeable when selection is weak. A gene for a trait not under selection can drift randomly in frequency across generations to the point where everyone in the population has it—it becomes *fixed* in the population—or it disappears and no one has it. As we will see in a minute, cultural traits can drift in a parallel manner.

Drift also refers to chance events among organisms in a population that affect the frequencies of different kinds of traits, whether they are genetic or cultural. Let's say a female mountain lion in the western United States has the highest fitness of her population. She has keen eyesight, great sense of smell, and excellent mothering instincts. She doesn't let any other mountain lions, male or female, push her around; she can hunt practically blindfolded; and she's produced two cubs that look to be exact miniatures of her. Even though she exhibits a general distrust of males, her sleek fur and other outward signals of fecundity nevertheless make her the ideal mate, and all the males know it—as do the jealous females. One day, our lioness is out hunting on a high rise, when a thunderstorm appears, and lightning suddenly strikes and kills her. This is what we mean by the "chance component" of evolution. Even though in terms of fitness our lioness was at the top of the heap, a random event took her out. Selection played no role in this evolutionary outcome. Notice that in our example the lioness had produced two offspring, which would carry her excellent genes into the next generation, provided they themselves make it. If, however, we take away the lion cubs, her fit gene line goes extinct, all because of a chance bolt of lightning.

What does all this mean for humans and the decisions we make? The same evolutionary processes at work in the biological realm are also at work in the cultural realm. Cultural selection is just like biological selection in its effect on descent with modification, just as cultural drift is akin to biological drift. To make the point, let's take a look at two fictional case studies, both of which center on guys in bars. In the first scenario, our character is in his twenties, single, and (sort of) looking for a girlfriend. He still lives with his parents and works at the local hardware store. He knows, though, that it pays to stand out from the crowd, so when he gets up in the morning he puts on a bright red polyester shirt, unbuttoned to show his chest hair and gold chains, pulls the shirt collar outside his black leather jacket, and squeezes into tight black trousers. Stepping into his shiny red boots, he's ready to start the day, strutting down the sidewalk, smiling (and leering) at every woman he walks by. After work, he returns to his parent's basement, changes into pink polyester

Source: Courtesy of Paramount Pictures

pants, a print shirt, and a red leather jacket and wears these, again with his red boots and gold chains, to the local nightclub.

When girls at the club see him, do they swoon around him, or do they freak out and pepper-spray him? The answer depends, of course, when this occurred. We've just described John Travolta's character, Tony Manero, in *Saturday Night Fever*, which appeared in 1977, the height of the disco era. His outfit and attitude certainly worked then because everyone more or less dressed that way. If a young man were to repeat this now, however, he might not leer at women on the street although he might wear some of the same clothes but do it in a way that shows that he knows he's being campy. Or, a guy might wear the same outfit in earnest, professing loudly Travolta's greatness as an actor. In either case, the goal is to be charmingly or interestingly abnormal—one standard deviation from the mean—without being a nutjob outlier—four standard deviations from the mean, where you're liable to get pepper-sprayed.

The point is, clothes are necessary, but attractiveness is a moving target that changes with time. Clothes in general are an adaptation, with features that increase our fitness—keeping us from freezing to death and, importantly, keeping us in the breeding population. You might be warm enough whether you wear polyester stretch pants, silk netherstocks, or wool trousers, but for attracting a potential mate, both time and place will matter. Reproductive fitness expressed through fashion is not the same as staying warm. Modern fashions are subject to drift—the color, material, and style are rarely driven by selection. At one level, we are "selecting"—making decisions about—what to wear, but the choices from which we select have been prechosen by clothing designers and market researchers. Here, drift is not truly "random"—although we say it is for simplicity's sake—because there is a limited range of choices as opposed to an infinite number. Designers and marketers know what sells and what doesn't.

Prehistoric clothing, however, was governed by a different balance of drift and selection. We get a vivid sense of this from so-called "bog bodies" preserved in archaeology. In the summer of 1370 BC, near what is now Egtved, Denmark, a young Nordic Bronze Age woman was buried in an oak coffin wearing a short tunic made of woven imported wool, a knee-length skirt made of twisted wool yarns, a woven wool belt, a bronze belt plate decorated with spirals, an earring, and a hairnet. Which of these objects were under selection, and which were subject to drift? The use of wool was under selection, not only because wool keeps you warm even when it's wet but also because sheep herding had been an adaptive practice in northern Europe for thousands of years. But the short cut of the tunic or the spirals on the bronze belt plate? They might have been the fashion of the Nordic Bronze Age.

Let's leave Denmark and go back to our mythical American nightclub, which has now become a country-and-western dance hall. We'll introduce two bartenders, courtesy of a story told by one of Mike's long-time friends and collaborators, archaeologist Bob Leonard. Both bartenders are among the best there are. They pay attention to orders, they're great conversationalists, and they know when to shut people off who have had too much to drink. And they love busy nights because of the tips. Actually, everything about the two is identical, except for one seemingly small detail. One bartender opens beer bottles with a church key, whereas the other one uses an old-fashioned opener mounted on the back of the long bar, just above the sink. At first glance, why would this make the slightest difference in terms of fitness? Both guys can use either implement to open a beer bottle and slide it down to the customer. Wouldn't the decision as to which one to use be purely random—a product of drift? Surely it couldn't have an effect on a bartender's fitness because, after all, a beer opener is a beer opener. In addition to the various shapes and sizes of church keys, there are the gimmick openers that liquor stores give away, Swiss army knives, and even the interior lock of a pickup truck.

As Bob explained it, for most of us, how efficient one kind of opener is compared to another really doesn't matter much because we're going to open only a few beers at a time. One might work better than another at the backyard grill, perhaps another on a picnic, and so on, but again, because we're opening only a few bottles, the choice of one over another is not going to affect our fitness. But what about bartenders? Let's call on Bob's two characters to help us figure that out. We notice that over the course of an evening, Jared, using the opener mounted behind the bar, opens six beers per minute, with an average 10-cent tip for each beer served. That's $36 an hour and $216 for a six-hour shift. Ronnie, who uses a church key, opens five beers per minute, which means he's 17 percent less efficient. We might ask, "So? That's a pretty small difference." Let's keep going. Tips are the same, so Ronnie receives $30 an hour and $180 for the shift—$36 less than Jared.

Our bartenders allow us to extend our experiment for a year, and assuming each works the standard 260 workdays in a work year, Jared will have earned $9,360 more than Ronnie. Now we're talking real money. At the end of the experiment, we find that Ronnie has been unable to adequately feed and clothe his family, and many of his bills have gone unpaid. His wife has left him, and creditors are beating down his door, all because he used a technology that was "only" 17 percent less efficient than what his friend used, who, by the way, is driving a new Lexus, with a pretty, not to mention pregnant, wife by his side. Jared drives his kid to private school in a Range Rover, while Ronnie has no kids at home because his wife took them with her. He wonders whether filing for bankruptcy might stop the robocalls from debt collectors for the Buick he financed.

Bob's point is, cumulatively over time, small differences—a technology "only" 17 percent more efficient—can have real fitness effects. In our imaginary scenario, the efficiency translated into tip money, but it could just as easily translate into energy savings. They would be small for each opening event, but over a lifetime, consuming energy that could potentially be used for other purposes, including reproduction and parental investment in offspring, might be important. When technology inherited from previous generations affects birth rate, it is creating an evolutionary effect. Imagine a Neolithic village of a hundred people who cultivate einkorn wheat, which allows their population to grow at 1 percent per year. Villagers 50 kilometers upriver, however, herd cattle, and not only do they drink milk and eat cheese, but they trade their surplus cheese for wheat, which they use to make bread. This village grows at 2 percent annually. Everything being equal, after a century, the cattle herders will well outnumber the wheat farmers. Ignore for now other factors we'll discuss in later chapters, such as migration and copying the success of your neighbors. The point here is that slight changes in decisions and associated behaviors might allow one group to outcompete another one. Neither group may even recognize that it's taking place. Again, individual decisions, when aggregated, can have major evolutionary implications.

ECONOMIC TERMS

Most behavioral sciences have flourished by studying, or at least assuming, how relatively well-informed individuals normally act in their own self-interest. This perspective has its roots in early economics—Adam's Smith's *Wealth of Nations*, published in 1776, was famously built on the notion of self-interest. John Stuart Mill wrote in 1836 that the field of political economy "is concerned with [man] solely as a being who desires to possess wealth, and who is capable of judging the comparative efficacy of means for obtaining that end." By this he meant "with the smallest quantity of labour and physical self-denial." Mill's perspective came to be known colloquially as *Homo economicus*—"Economic man"—by some of his late-nineteenth-century critics who doubted that humans had perfect control over risk, reward, and the amount of labor involved for an intended outcome. While no one ever really thought people were such omniscient, optimality-calculating deciders, there is considerable debate over how useful *rational decision-making* is as a basic economic assumption. Over the last twenty years, for example, the Nobel Prize winners in economics have held very different positions on this fundamental issue.

Three economic terms are important here: *utility, search goods,* and *experience goods.* These concepts behind the terms can get complicated mathematically, but we aim for simplicity here. Utility refers to preferences. For example, do you prefer chocolate milk or white milk? How much more do you prefer one than the other? These questions assume you are free to decide between the two with no constraints. If someone else is buying, maybe you ask for the more expensive chocolate milk, whereas at the supermarket, you buy white milk because you decide chocolate milk is not worth the extra price. In this sense, utility is the satisfaction we get from buying something or doing something. People will pay fifty times more to go to a Dallas Cowboys game than to the movies if they feel they get fifty times the satisfaction from the game. This is the *utility function*: faced with a set of options and a limited budget, we decide on the option that leads to the greatest satisfaction. Although we can't actually observe the utility function in the human mind—neuroscientists, however, are making progress on this—economists use proxies for it by way of behavior, such as tabulating items in a consumer's shopping cart.

Search goods are those where the consumer already knows the payoff, so he or she searches for the lowest price—hence the term "search goods." Sales of cheap alcoholic beverages, such as 40-ounce cans of malt liquor, often reflect how drunk you can get for the price. A friend of Alex's who received his medical degree from Brown University decided to take over the family business of converting recycled paper products into such things as paper towels for auto shops and toilet paper for buses. A medical doctor who had once flown to India to assist in an emergency, he said his most exciting task now was measuring the thickness of rolled paper with calipers. No matter how the product was packaged, how absorbent it was, what the texture was, or how it was marketed, his clients consistently asked only one question: how much? That was the be-all and end-all of their purchasing decision, so price per pound—hence, the calipers—was all the company focused on (this friend has since launched a start-up in Silicon Valley and is much happier).

As opposed to search goods, where you know equivalencies and are searching for the lowest price, maybe you need to try something out in order to discover whether there's a bigger payoff to using that item as opposed to a familiar item. Or maybe you copy experienced users whose preferences are like yours. Such a good is termed an *experience good*. Producers know that consumers do not have all the needed information to make a choice, and they keep prices fairly consistent across the marketplace out of fear that a dramatically lower price than what the competition is offering may signal lower quality. It's seemingly much tougher for a consumer to compare health-insurance plans than it is to compare toothpaste although both actions are decision based. For us, how the decisions are made is what's important. What about goods where even after experiencing them, the consumer can't figure out what the payoff is? These are called *postexperience goods*, and supplement companies make fortunes off of them. So, too, do private ratings companies, as opposed to government agencies such as the US Food and Drug Administration, which provide third-party information as a public service.

OK; enough terms and definitions for now. We'll introduce more as we go along, but these will serve to get us started. Let's turn the page and take a brief look at how decisions get formed in the first place.

TEAMS AND FITNESS

Decisions start in the mind, but what distinguishes the mind from the brain? Plato and Aristotle wrestled with this, as have philosophers, mathematicians, psychologists, anthropologists, and neurobiologists. At a perspective of 30,000 feet, we see the *brain* as the physical matter—a three-pound mass of gray matter, to be specific—that uses 100 billion neurons, each of which has some 7,000 synaptic connections to other neurons, in order to organize and process what the *mind* sends it in terms of thoughts, beliefs, judgments and biases, perceptions, and memories. Decision-making, which takes place in the prefrontal cortex, along with other executive functions, is the cognitive process that calls on beliefs, memories, and the like; uses them to produce possible courses of action; and then selects from among the alternatives. Although often thought of in this way, the mind is not simply an expression of the brain by itself but an expression of the entire body. It would be sheer reductionism to say, for example, that hunger in the stomach elicits a direct response from the brain. Rather, hunger elicits a response from the mind in terms of decision-making, which *takes place* in the prefrontal cortex portion of the brain.

On a short and stressful break from work, we might, for example, choose a ready-made 1,340-calorie Monster Thickburger at Hardee's rather than carrots and tofu from the corner grocery. On the weekend, with more time to think about our choice, we might settle on a juicy grilled steak, remembering how good the last one was, and plan to invite some friends over to share it. This ability to weigh a multitude of options and plan ahead sets humans apart from other organisms, at least as far as we know. Set down a bowl of Alpo, and your dog comes running; there's no planning ahead or inviting other dogs over to share it. For human groups, however, planning to eat can be complicated, depending on the social context. In traditional societies, for example, food decisions can have great significance, where sharing food can facilitate alliances, promote the provider's prestige, or exercise power over others.

If the mind, rather than the brain, makes decisions—selecting one choice from among alternatives—then group minds, as on a team or committee, might qualify as a collective mind, arriving at a collective decision. Good leaders understand and often manage how each individual contributes to the group decision—the ideas person, the details person, the naysayer, the agree-with-the-last-suggestion person, and so on. Whether in a boardroom or on a basketball court, an individual's fitness depends in part on the fitness of his or her teammates. And, of course, the fitness of the team is a composite of individual fitnesses. We'll come back to the important distinction between individuals and groups of individuals later in the chapter, asking whether a team has properties outside of the summed aggregate properties of individuals. Here, though, we want to observe how individual players can affect a team when they decide to join or leave it. Let's use professional basketball as an example. Tamika Catchings, WNBA Rookie of the Year in 2002, is an interesting case. She led the Indiana Fever to win 50 percent of its games that year, compared with 31 percent the year before (Catchings was coached by Pat Summitt, perhaps the greatest coach ever, at the University of Tennessee). In her last season, 2016, the Fever won 50 percent of its games, but the following year, the team won only 26 percent. Similarly, the season after they drafted LeBron James in 2003, the Cleveland Cavaliers of the NBA won 43 percent of their games, compared to 21 percent the season before. When James was traded to the Miami Heat in 2010, the Cavaliers fell from a 74 percent winning percentage to a dismal 23 percent, and the Heat improved from 57 percent to 70 percent. When the Cavaliers got James back in 2014–2015, Cleveland improved from 40 percent to 64 percent, whereas the Miami Heat fell from 66 percent to 45 percent. It's pretty clear how important certain individuals can be to a team.

Still, there is "no single metric wholly predictive of success," as one study of NBA teams found. Why is it so hard to predict who will win? It's doubtful that anyone really could have predicted how much Tamika Catchings or LeBron James would improve their respective teams before these great players actually started playing for them. Success on a new team is just not easily predicted. Indeed, plenty of highly touted college athletes, even Heisman winners such as Johnny Manziel and Tim Tebow, were unsuccessful in the NFL. Conversely, many of the greatest professional players—quarterbacks Tom Brady, Brett Favre, and Kurt Warner, for example—were unexceptional in college. Let's take a closer look at NFL quarterbacks and the decisions they make, as well as at aggregate decisions at the level of the teams that draft them. Before we're done, we'll reintroduce two topics from the last chapter—selection and fitness—and see how they apply at the two levels. Specifically, does selection operate only at the level of individuals, or can it operate at the group level as well?

MORE THAN THROWING DEEP

America has a love affair with quarterbacks because they are the face of a football team. Quarterbacks not only lead teams but also steer their personalities. If someone is not a leader, he won't last long as a quarterback. That goes for pee-wee football as well as the NFL. Despite being centers of attention, quarterbacks might, on average, have better physiques because of strict diet and exercise, but then again, if we surveyed a hundred males at our local Gold's Gym, only one of whom was an NFL quarterback, we probably would be hard-pressed to pick him out. And if you grew up in the 1960s, you might remember the likes of the Washington Redskins' Sonny Jurgensen and Billy Kilmer, whose considerable paunches were no different from those of their loyal meat-loving, beer-chugging fans. Back in those days, the public had few, if any, options for working out other than at the YMCA, and on the NFL side, the players avoided exercise at all costs. It worked out just fine.

Decisions that players make, both on and off the field, have tremendous effects on a team's success, which is the reason that the NFL uses the Wonderlic Personnel Test as part of its annual predraft Scouting Combine, to which top prospects are invited to work out in front of all 32 teams. In today's highly complicated and fast-paced offenses, it's great to have a quarterback who can throw 70 yards on a rope and run at least a respectable 4.8-second 40-yard dash, but he also has to absorb vast amounts of information and be able to recall it quickly. The Wonderlic, which lasts only twelve minutes and has fifty questions, isn't a surefire test of excellent decision-making, and in fact, in his book *How We Decide*, Jonah Lehrer concluded that the test does not predict the success of an NFL quarterback in the least because finding an open receiver is different than solving an algebra problem. After all, Pittsburgh's Terry Bradshaw scored a 16, and he won all four Super Bowls in which he appeared. We get Lehrer's point, but as we point out later, evolution just might quibble with him.

DRAFTING TOM BRADY

In deciding on which players to draft, especially quarterbacks, NFL personnel face tough and often gut-wrenching decisions, especially with the "you'd-better-win-it-all-today" mentality of NFL fans. There are only seven rounds in the NFL draft, meaning each team gets seven picks, although it could be higher or lower, depending on trades and the like. Given all the time that the 32 teams put into scouting prospects in terms of speed, coordination, strength, intelligence, and character, the list of the supposedly best players will be quite similar from one team to another. Things change quickly, though, as the draft starts and players' names keep dropping off the board. This is where you'd better have a plan B—and a plan C, and a plan D. To see where all this leads, let's go back to the 2000 draft and the New England Patriots. The Pats had just fired coach Pete Carroll at the end of the 1999 season, replacing him with Bill Belichick. The Patriots front office was high on a quarterback out of the University of Michigan, Tom Brady, whom they knew possessed leadership skills but questionable physical skills. He had lost his starting job at Michigan his senior year, and his showing at the Scouting Combine had been uninspiring, including running a 5.2-second 40-yard dash. Most linemen routinely turn in better times.

At the end of the draft, 254 players had been taken. The Patriots took Brady at number 199, the last pick in the sixth round. Six quarterbacks were drafted ahead of Brady. Ever heard of Spergon Wynn or Giovanni Carmazzi? What about Tee Martin? We didn't think so. Two of them never started an NFL game, and one, Wynn, started only three. Despite being a low draft pick, Brady turned out to be the greatest NFL quarterback of all time and certainly the biggest steal in NFL draft history, winning five Super Bowls (and counting), and coming in second in three more. Was it luck, hard work, or both? Certainly, luck played some role, in that another team could have picked him ahead of the Patriots. If they had, we might refer to that component as *drift*—the random occurrence in evolution that we mentioned in chapter 2. But what about *selection*, the nonrandom occurrence? Even if Jonah Lehrer is correct—that there is no correlation between the Wonderlic test and how well a quarterback makes decisions on the field—a high IQ can unquestionably preadapt individuals for certain activities. It doesn't mean they will be successful—quarterbacks need athletic ability as well as a drive to succeed—but any edge is useful in a competitive world. Selection and fitness work on slight edges, whether we're talking about NFL quarterbacks or, as we saw in chapter 2, bartenders who use different kinds of bottle openers.

With respect to Brady, his performance at the Scouting Combine waved off a lot of teams, and the Patriots gambled that he would still be around toward the end of the draft. A risky move, but the decision paid off because they were able to draft other players they needed ahead of him. What did the Patriots see that other teams didn't? Was there some hint of how good Brady would be? We probably will never know. In fact, Scott Pioli, assistant director of player personnel for the Patriots at the time, probably doesn't know. In hindsight, he might mention his intuition, or Brady's Wonderlic score of 33, which was higher (and in most cases considerably higher) than the other six quarterbacks selected before him. Again, as Lehrer points out, that kind of score doesn't ensure success at the NFL level, but again, selection works on edges, and *that's* what matters. In Brady's

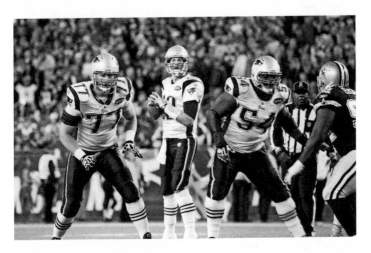

Source: Courtesy of Joseph Sohm, Shutterstock

case, that edge was a very good intellect and a knowledge of the game, which he honed through thousands of hours of practice and film watching.

In taking Brady, Pioli and the Patriots threw some long-standing economic principles out the window, substituting intuition (or whatever other behavior they used) for rational expectations and efficient markets. A fascinating behavioral economic look at how NFL teams draft was provided by economists Cade Massey and Richard Thaler in a paper with the provocative title "The Loser's Curse." Their premise was that psychological factors lead teams to overvalue the chance to pick early in the draft, and thus they trade up, often giving away tons of lower picks and even picks in future years. Massey and Thaler used data on draft-day trades, player performance, and compensation and compared the market value of draft picks to the surplus value to teams provided by the drafted players. Sure enough, they found that top draft picks are significantly overvalued. This behavior wouldn't happen in efficient markets.

The research caught the attention of NFL owners, one of whom, the Washington Redskins' Daniel Snyder, was eager to hear Thaler's strategy and actually discussed it with him. Snyder later had some of his player personnel follow up with the economist. Apparently, it didn't matter what they did or didn't learn because Snyder never took the future Nobel laureate's advice, always trading high picks in a scramble for immediate success, which almost never came (four playoff appearances in the eighteen years Snyder has owned the team). As an example, in the 2012 draft, Washington dealt first- and second-round picks for that year plus first-round picks for 2013 and 2014 to the Rams for the number 2 overall pick, which they used on Robert Griffin III, who had had a phenomenal career as a quarterback at Baylor. After his great rookie season, though, he tore an ACL and has never been the same. Given all the draft picks they continue to give up, neither have the Redskins. (NFL owner's note to self: stockpile second- and third-round picks to counter the effects of drift, which can knock out a star athlete the same as it did the female cougar from chapter 2.)

NEUROPLASTICITY AND LONDON TAXI DRIVERS

Here's an interesting thought: can the decisions we make, especially if they are continually reinforced, leave detectable changes in the brain? We know, of course, that the brain exhibits *neuroplasticity*, meaning that it can change both its structure and function in response to real as well as imagined experience, but can it change in some physically recognizable way? Will learning complicated NFL offenses, especially elaborate passing routes, lead to physical changes in a quarterback's brain that we can actually see? We're not sure, but let's look for clues in the brains of London taxi drivers. To earn a license to drive a cab in central London, one has to have "The Knowledge," which is a complex mental map of a six-mile radius around Charing Cross train station that contains an estimated 25,000 streets and alleys, not to mention thousands of hotels, theaters, restaurants, and landmarks. After four years of training, which involves learning the 320 routes listed in the "Blue Book," plus all the roads and landmarks within a quarter-mile radius of the start and end points of each route, applicants have to stand for a series of rigorous examinations in front of master cabdrivers who can ask them the tiniest of details in terms of how to get from point A to point B in the shortest amount of time. It is an exercise that is unique among taxi drivers anywhere in the world, and it has been in place since 1865.

In 2000, Eleanor Maguire and her colleagues at University College London began neuroimaging a group of taxi drivers in training, comparing magnetic resonance images of their brains to their performance on memory tasks. They found that having a highly complex mental map of London corresponded with higher gray-matter volume in the *posterior hippocampus*, that portion of the brain where short-term information is consolidated into long-term memory and where spatial navigation is controlled. Conversely, no structural brain changes were observed in trainees who failed to qualify or in control participants. Neither were they found in bus drivers, who follow prescribed routes as opposed to having to make on-the-spot decisions as to what the shortest route is between two points.

It's not just that people with a large hippocampus are predisposed to drive taxis. Rather, driving a taxi appears to increase gray-matter volume of the hippocampus, given the positive correlation between hippocampal gray-matter volume and *years* of taxi driving, with those gains being gradually lost after a taxi driver retires. There may be a price connected to acquiring this spatial knowledge of London, perhaps a reduction in anterior hippocampal volume. In tests, taxi drivers tended to exhibit poorer learning and memory for certain types of new visual information, such as delayed recall of complex figures.

As Maguire and her colleagues note, these findings have significance for the "nature versus nurture" debate, in that they indicate that specific, long-lasting structural changes in the brain can be induced by biologically relevant behaviors that engage higher cognitive functions such as spatial memory. They also provide insight into the boundaries within which human decision-making operates. There are strong parallels between learning which London streets go where and learning how each of your receivers and backs run pass routes out of various offensive sets. Like a London taxi driver, Tom Brady has "The Knowledge." We're not sure what changes Tom Brady's brain might have made over the course of his career, but we can make an educated guess: a selective increase in gray-matter volume in the posterior hippocampus.

IFS AND BUTS

It's incredible how one set of decisions can create so many outcomes if one decision is tweaked in even the tiniest way. If we replayed the tape of life, things would turn out differently. Paleobiologist Stephen Jay Gould made that point with respect to the Middle Cambrian fauna in the Burgess Shale of western Canada in his 1989 book, *Wonderful Life*. Gould cleverly borrowed the title from the Frank Capra 1946 movie, *It's a Wonderful Life*, in which an angel takes the guy played by Jimmy Stewart, who is contemplating suicide, back in time to show him how different life would have been had he not been born. Gould's point was that if we could go back 500 million years and make slight environmental changes so that just one or two genera of Cambrian fauna didn't appear, how would life have turned out? Or suppose we could halt large-scale events, such as sea slides, that wiped out dozens of genera? How would life have turned out then? Would we even be here today? His point was that life is not a series of random events. Rather, it's a continuum of contingencies, meaning that each step along the way is contingent on what came before. Can we always see these steps? No, of course not. But philosopher Dan Dennett makes an excellent point with respect to the power of Darwin's theory of natural selection, noting that its power lies not in its ability to prove exactly how history was but in its power to show how it *could* have been, given a certain set of conditions.

Contingencies underlie every decision we make, whether at the individual level—you decide to buy a car—or at the collective level—we all start shopping on Amazon. And those decisions can often—probably more often than we think—affect fitness. The question is, can it work at the group level as well as at the individual level? At the individual level, Tom Brady's fitness was certainly affected by being drafted by the New England Patriots, whose owner, Robert Kraft, and the Patriots front office were ready to spend the cash to build a winning team. What if the Cleveland Browns had used the 183rd pick overall and taken Brady instead of Spergon Wynn? Would Brady have had the same success in Cleveland he's had in New England? Would he have made $200 million with the Browns as he has with the Patriots—the third highest behind Peyton and Eli Manning? Would he have met, let alone married, supermodel Gisele Bündchen—who herself brings in around $47 million a year—and had two beautiful kids, in addition to the son he already had? Would he own a mansion in Brookline, Massachusetts, and a penthouse in Manhattan? Or, like our bartender Ronnie in chapter 2, would he be wifeless and childless and drive a Buick that he financed?

We'll never know, but why should we even care what *might* have happened? It's sort of like what Don Meredith, the long-time quarterback of the Dallas Cowboys, once said when he cohosted *Monday Night Football*: "If 'ifs' and 'buts' were candy and nuts, wouldn't it be a Merry Christmas?" What we *do* know is that playing for the Patriots has affected Brady's fitness in a positive way, and that's really all that matters. And, it appears that it has also affected the fitness of the Patriots, including adding to owner Robert Kraft's $4 billion net worth. This brings up a fascinating topic that will stay with us throughout the book to one degree or another: group selection.

WHY ONLY INDIVIDUALS?

Perhaps no topic in evolutionary biology incites more debate—sometimes downright nasty debate—than group fitness. Why would this be the case? Can't behaviors benefit both the individual and the group? Some biologists and philosophers, such as E. O. Wilson and Elliott Sober, would say yes, but many more would echo what Harvard psychologist Steven Pinker had to say: "[G]roup selection has no useful role to play in psychology or social science. If a person has innate traits that encourage him to contribute to the group's welfare and as a result contribute to *his own* welfare, group selection is unnecessary; individual selection in the context of group living is adequate."

Biologist George Williams used deer to point out the difference between individual and group selection. Think of a herd of fleet deer versus a fleet herd of deer. They are not the same thing. In the first, individual deer can usually outrun predators much more easily than deer outside the herd. Thus, in terms of fitness, we might want to claim that our herd of fleet deer is more fit than other herds—and will become even more fleet because the deer within it escape predation and produce more offspring over time. But there's a catch here: selection, in one sense, obviously works in the herd's favor, but we can't say that the herd has properties that are somehow different from those of the aggregated individuals. In other words, fleetness is an adaptation that evolved to benefit *individual* deer, not the group of which they are a member. However, with respect to Pinker's point above, a fleet deer contributes to the herd's welfare because his or her genes have a better chance of being passed on.

No doubt Tom Brady's fitness was enhanced by being drafted by the Patriots. As we saw, he started with an edge—a selective advantage in terms of intellect and drive—and it got sharper through time, both because he worked endlessly to make himself better—a conscious decision—and because he was surrounded by excellent personnel, both on and off the field. At the same time, the fitness of others in the Patriot organization increased *relative to individuals in other NFL organizations* by drafting Brady and surrounding him with highly skilled personnel, resulting in five Super Bowl trophies and sellout crowds every year since 1994, the year Kraft assumed ownership. That's 261 consecutive games, not counting preseason and postseason games, all of which also sold out.

Obviously, what's good for Brady is good for the Patriots—as long as he stays healthy and performs well—but let's bear in mind that what's good for the Patriots is also good for Brady. Somewhere in all the discussion of group selection lurks the notion of "altruism," which many biologists and behavioral scientists dismiss. They argue that what appear to be acts of altruism are really decisions that affect the fitness of the one committing the act. It's hard to escape the veracity of that statement. We can think of only a few examples that might qualify—maybe a soldier falling on a grenade (although we could take the other side in that one) or leaving a waitress a $100 tip, knowing you'll never see her again—but at best, those are exceptions that prove the rule. There is an evolutionary alternative to the argument that John Terra made in a post on his website, FanRag Sports, in January 2015. A week earlier, Brady had decided to restructure his deal with the Patriots and free up $24 million so it could be used to buy other players. As Terra noted, this was a risk on Brady's part because the Patriots no longer faced any monetary penalty for cutting him. He wrote, "[T]he New England Patriots have to be so thankful for the fact that they have Tom Brady. Not only because he won them three Super Bowls and got them to another two, but because he may be one of the nicest guys in existence. Very few players will give up guaranteed money not once, but twice—especially when it is millions of dollars." We don't doubt that Tom Brady *is* a nice guy, but from an evolutionary standpoint he made an individual decision that, if he stayed healthy, could gain him a whole lot more money than $24 million over the next chapter of his career. He would never have to worry about driving a used Buick like Ronnie the bartender. Again, what's good for the Patriots is good for Brady. That has nothing to do with being a nice guy, but it has everything to do with being a smart guy.

As a way of wrapping up our discussion of group fitness, let's leave it at this: decisions that individuals make can affect not only their fitness but the fitness of others in their group. That way, we don't have to worry about whether "group selection" exists or not. Similarly, collective decisions can affect individual fitness. O. J. Simpson may or may not have decided to kill Nicole Brown Simpson and Ron Goldman—the criminal-trial jury said no, the civil-trial jury said he was liable (not the same thing as being found guilty)—but the collective groups that heard the evidence reached decisions that clearly affected his fitness. And not only that, the decisions had far-flung ramifications on the fitness of others, including the families of the victims, the careers of the prosecutors, and the downstream fortunes of the defense-team members.

As we pointed out at the beginning of this chapter, decision-making is the cognitive process that uses judgment, biases, beliefs, and other mental abstractions to lay out possibilities for a course of action. Where do these abstractions come from, and how are they honed over time? The answer is, they come from learning—the fundamental input process that fills the mind with data for the brain to organize. Let's turn the page and take a look at the various and distinct kinds of learning that are involved.

4

HOW DO WE LEARN?

In the 1976 movie *Logan's Run*, which is set in the year 2274, Logan and Jessica are running from the domed, hedonistic city where their blissful lives would have been mandatorily terminated at age 30. Entering an ice cave outside the city, they encounter a British robot named Box, which looks like a vacuum cleaner. "Fish, and plankton," says Box robotically, "and sea greens, and protein from the sea." Box then tries to freeze-dry Logan and Jessica to add to his purposeless seafood supply for a human culture that presumably went extinct long ago.

Logan's Run is part of the science-fiction genre exploring dystopian scenarios of future cultural evolution that dates back at least to H. G. Wells's 1895 book, *The Time Machine*. In popular media, cultural evolution is often viewed as a progression in a discernable direction, although, as we saw in chapter 2, cultural evolution is just a process that sorts variation over time. When some variants, or traits, are superior to others in terms of the fitness they confer on their bearers, they are sorted by natural selection as they are being passed from one generation to another. Over time, this process weeds out less fit individuals from the population. In *Logan's Run*, Box apparently viewed this as his personal responsibility.

But because all he "learned" was what was fed to him through a program, Box couldn't adjust to new information from the outside. He overloaded, which caused the end of the domed city. Organisms, however, fare much better—at least most do—because they can learn. Humans, of course, are the consummate learners. For our purposes, we divide learning into two categories, social learning and individual learning. This division is useful as long as we remember that humans are neither purely social nor purely individual learners, or, as our colleague Alex Mesoudi refers to them, *information scroungers* and *information producers*. Rather, certain conditions, perceived or real, dictate which type of learning might be more useful in any particular situation. Let's start with individual learning.

INDIVIDUAL LEARNING

Learning on our own—what we'll refer to as *individual learning*—is a slow process wherein an individual, through trial and error, modifies existing behaviors to suit his or her own needs. Maybe you observe the basic behavior from a parent or master and then begin to tinker with it with little or no influence from other people. For example, you might get a set of golf clubs for your birthday, but you live way out in the country, far from a golf course, and you don't know anyone who plays golf, much less teaches it. You practice by yourself day in and day out, reading a little about the different golf clubs and discovering through trial and error that hitting a golf ball requires a different swing than hitting a baseball—something you never would have figured out just by watching golfer John Daly, who models his swing after Babe Ruth's.

Rob Boyd and Pete Richerson refer to this as "guided variation," meaning that any variation—improvement in your golf swing, for example—is guided primarily by the individual with little or no outside influence. We call this form of learning *unbiased* because at the population level, which is what we're interested in, it approximately replicates the distribution of behaviors from the previous generation. Again, behaviors at the individual level are what create population-level behaviors, but they're changing so slowly—a slight variation here, another one there—that we barely notice any change in *overall* behavior from one generation to the next.

As a strategy, you might, before acquiring a behavior, scan the environment—cultural as well as physical—and see if you can glean any information about the relative payoffs of particular behaviors. If the difference in payoffs is clear—not a certainty in most situations—you adopt the behavior indicated by the environmental information. For example, let's say we're prehistoric hunters living in a regional environment that, over the generations, is changing from forest to open savannah. Along with that change is a gradual turnover in fauna, from fairly solitary browsers such as deer to herds of grazers such as bison and antelope. We then begin to modify our weaponry accordingly. For example, our previously used spears, which were adapted for closed-canopy environments, might no longer be useful in open terrain, where the animals can see us and run away. Maybe now we need lighter spears and points so that we can launch them from greater distances.

Back to scanning the horizon: maybe the payoff differences aren't readily obvious, so you just stick with your current behavior. Thus, guided variation has two equally important components: the individual-level learning process, which may occur many times per generation, and its transgenerational counterpart, *guided variation* (unbiased transmission and individual learning). Both are important components of individual decision-making. Interesting examples of unbiased learning occur when humans interact with other species. Take, for example, Koko, the female western lowland gorilla whose instructor and care giver, Penny Patterson, claimed the animal knew over a thousand hand signs of "Gorilla Sign Language" in addition to 2,000 spoken English words. There's also Betsy, a Viennese border collie that knows over three hundred words, and Chaser,

Source: Courtesy of Manuela Hartling, Reuters

a border collie that has a vocabulary of over a thousand words. Our favorite wonder animal, though, is Rico, a border collie—sadly, he died in 2008—studied by Juliane Kaminski and her colleagues at the Max Planck Institute for Evolutionary Anthropology in Leipzig, Germany.

When acquiring speech, children form quick and rough hypotheses about the meaning of a new word after only a single exposure—a process dubbed "fast mapping." Kaminski and colleagues' research suggested that Rico, too, was able to fast map. He knew the labels of over two hundred different items—he's shown in the photograph alongside some of his favorites—and, even more amazing, he inferred the names of novel items by exclusion learning. When asked, Rico could retrieve a new object that was placed alongside seven familiar ones. In human terms, he would scan the objects and think to himself, "Hmmm. I know the names of those seven objects, but I've never seen the one on the end. That must be the one they're talking about."

Rico was some smart dog, but how do "smart" animals compare to humans? Psychologist Paul Bloom points out that children have a diverse vocabulary, with names for people, objects, actions, and the like, whereas Rico knew words only for fetchable things such as balls and toys. Also, a nine-year-old human knows tens of thousands of words and picks up more than ten new words a day, whereas Rico knew two hundred. But still, Rico appreciated that new words referred to objects that for him did not already have names. Young children understand this as well. "Perhaps Rico is doing precisely what a child does, just not as well, Bloom wrote. "A 2-year-old human knows more than a 9-year-old dog, after all, and has a better memory, and a better ability to understand the minds of adults. Rico's limitations might reflect differences in degree, not in kind." We could not agree more.

SOCIAL LEARNING

Rico learned individually from his trainers, but if he had not been raised in a laboratory, he would have learned socially from other dogs. Organisms use *social learning* for all kinds of adaptive reasons, perhaps the most significant being that it gives them the ability to monitor the behavior of others in order to see what might be working and what isn't. This ability allows them to filter behaviors and adopt those that appear to have the highest payoffs. Copying confers adaptive plasticity not only on individuals but also on populations, allowing them to draw on deep knowledge bases in order to rapidly respond to changing environments. Copying is itself a set of competing strategies in that you might preferentially copy someone based on your perception of his or her skill level. Maybe you copy those who appear to be better at something than you are, or those who themselves appear to be good social learners, or those who are successful. Or maybe you base your decision on social criteria, so that you copy the majority of people you're around, or kin or friends, or older individuals. The various factors that can affect your choice of whom to copy are often referred to as "biases"—unique evolutionary forces for the selective retention of cultural variants. That's why the term "biased learning" is commonly used as a synonym for certain social-learning strategies.

The term "bias" is used in a statistical sense to indicate some deviation from random, or "unbiased," copying. There is a huge difference in the effects of copying based on knowledge or a skill level and copying based on random social interaction. Let's say you have a friend who excels as an investor—she loves to show you her E*TRADE accounts—and you follow the advice she gives you. That's biased learning. Conversely, putting the *New York Times* list of mutual funds on the wall and throwing a dart in order to pick one is not. Copying your investor friend is an example of *indirect bias*, in which learners use criteria such as success or prestige as a basis for selecting a model. Another kind of bias is *conformity bias*, or *frequency-dependent copying*, in which learners copy the most popular variant. We do this all the time. Imagine you're a new parent, walking into a day-care nursery where all the infants and toddlers are crawling around on the floor, with minimal supervision, doing one of two things: either sucking on a spoon or squishing some kind of slime into the floor. You want to buy something for your own child, but you can't ask the infants what's better, a spoon or the slime. Looking around, you see eight infants sucking on a spoon and only two squishing slime, so you use your phone to order a new spoon online. That's frequency-dependent bias. And by the way, Amazon already does this for you by ranking products by sales.

IMITATION VERSUS EMULATION

Dystopian tales, like *Logan's Run* or *Brave New World*, often depict the future as highly conformist, with everyone acting out a prescribed set of copied behaviors. What, exactly, is being copied? This is a crucial question for cultural evolution. Is it the set of behaviors that lead to something being produced or a decision being made, or is it the thing itself? This dichotomy is encapsulated in the distinction between *imitation*, copying the form of an action, versus *emulation*, copying the result of an action sequence. As clear-cut as this distinction sounds, how easy is it to apply in the field? Let's look at the well-documented case of macaque monkeys that live on Koshima, a small islet just off the west coast of Japan. One day in September 1953, a teacher who was assisting in provisioning the monkeys saw a young female, later named "Imo" (Japanese for "potato"), dipping sweet potatoes in water to get the sand off before she ate them. By all accounts, this seemed to be her original innovation, as no monkeys in the preceding years had been seen doing it. As opposed to Imo, when the other monkeys in her group ate sweet potatoes, they used their hands to knock off the sand. But once the others saw Imo washing the potatoes, the innovative behavior spread through the Koshima troop along two different channels, kinship relations and playmates. Imo's mother and siblings started first, then it was picked up by monkeys a year older or younger than Imo. By 1962, three-quarters of the troop over two years of age washed sweet potatoes. The washing was first done in the fresh water of a small stream, but during the course of transmission through generations, the monkeys started carrying the potatoes to the seashore. They not only washed the potatoes but also immersed them in the sea, perhaps to pick up the salt to enhance the flavor. Is this an example of imitation or of emulation? It's a little tough to say at this point, but let's look at another example.

Doree Fragaszy, who directs the Primate Cognition and Behavior Laboratory at the University of Georgia, has conducted long-term studies of another monkey genus, the bearded capuchins that live in the savannah of Brazil. One of the monkeys' economic pursuits involves cracking tough palm nuts using large stones as hammers and stone or log surfaces as anvils. This is no simple task, in that it involves proper stance, proper placement of a nut on an anvil, and a proper striking angle so that the nut doesn't skip away. Adults crack the nuts routinely throughout the year, but juveniles rarely manage to crack a whole nut, even though from a young age and for several years they devote considerable time and effort to watching their elders and practicing pounding actions with bits of nut and small stones. Adult monkeys tend to leave physical traces of nut cracking, including a fragrant oily residue on the stone tools and bits of kernel in cracked shells that litter the workplaces. Young monkeys are attracted to both, and they nibble at the contents and bang the shells on a convenient surface to knock loose another fragment of kernel.

Source: Courtesy of Barth Wright, EthoCebus Project

In addition, adults leave their tools around, which attracts the youngsters and probably adds to the developing scaffolding in their brains. Can young monkeys learn to crack nuts, or at least improve their technique, from directly copying some aspect of the behavior of others? It's tough to say, exactly. Here, beating on a nut because another monkey is pounding on one might increase the copier's skill, but simply pounding a stone on a nut is not sufficient to crack it. Fragaszy points out that even after a young monkey reliably produces all the relevant actions, and in the correct sequence, it takes another year or more before it succeeds in cracking a whole nut.

THE LEGENDARY SKILL OF WOODY THE FLINTKNAPPER

We would argue, as would most primatologists, that chimpanzees exhibit a rich mix of imitation and other forms of social learning, as well as individual learning. There is strong evidence to suggest that they select among these according to one or several factors that make the choice adaptive. One of the most fascinating examples of this mix of copying strategies comes not from chimpanzees but from humans, and it involves the purchase of a bunch of Clovis spearpoints, which were used by big-game hunters who roamed North America between about 13,300 and 12,500 years ago. The stone points are lanceolate in shape and have parallel to slightly convex sides, concave bases, and short basal flutes that extend a quarter to a third the length of a point. Making a Clovis point is a complex procedure that would have required a significant amount of investment both in terms of time and energy to learn effectively. Thus, we would guess that there was significant variation among the level of skill exhibited by toolmakers, and perhaps recognized craftsmen could have held considerable prestige.

Source: Courtesy of Charlotte Pevny and the Center for the Study of the First Americans

Clovis points can sell on the artifact market anywhere from a few hundred dollars up to $50,000 or more for extremely large, beautiful examples. Years ago, an artifact collector in New Mexico bought several Clovis points that ostensibly came out of a cache of points that had been found years earlier, paying an extraordinary sum of money for them. Before buying them, he had a number of knowledgeable collectors and archaeologists look at them, and they all blessed them as being the real deal. But they weren't. It turns out they were made by Woody Blackwell, who was well-known in the knapping world for his ability to make Clovis points as thin and beautiful as those of the original craftsmen. As models, Blackwell copied points from the Drake Clovis cache from Colorado. What eventually led to the realization that they were copies was the sharp eye of University of Cincinnati archaeologist Ken Tankersley, who saw tiny amounts of Georgia red clay in a few flake scars. He realized that Blackwell had used the clay as a buffer in a rock tumbler, gently rolling the points around to knock off sharp edges of the flake scars. On authentic points, the natural elements, over thousands of years, do the work of a rock tumbler. It later was shown that Blackwell had used a Brazilian quartz as his raw material, but at the time of sale, people figured the source was just a previously unknown one from somewhere in western North America. Everybody knew Blackwell was good, but was he really *that* good to have fooled experts? Apparently so.

As interesting as the story is, it gets even better. Years later, Sabrina Sholts, who works at the Smithsonian's National Museum of Natural History, and several of her colleagues wanted to see how standardized Clovis flaking was across North America. The shape of Clovis points can differ significantly from region to region, but no one had ever measured variation in flake scars. The research group developed a novel and sophisticated method of measuring the shape of flake scars and tried it out on thirty-nine authentic Clovis points.

Just for the heck of it, they added in eleven of Blackwell's replicas. After scanning the points, they used a sorting method, *principal components analysis*, to pull out the variables that caused the most deviation among the flake-scar contours. Most contours, irrespective of the region of North America from which the points came, clustered in a tight pattern, but several of them were way outside the cluster. Guess which points they represented? Yep; Woody Blackwell's. Not all of them were extreme outliers, but a number were. This was because Blackwell could sometimes replicate the flake-removal pattern of a Clovis knapper, but he was inconsistent in his ability to do so. As Blackwell later told a reporter, "I just stopped and looked at [a] piece and said, 'That really looks like a Drake-style Clovis if I stop right there.' Until then, I had always kept going, cleaning up the edges, making the point smoother, getting the symmetry dead on, and really dressing the thing up. What I'd been losing was its immediacy, its simplicity."

Of course, the real reason for his failure to consistently match the flaking pattern was because Blackwell was born 13,000 years too late to have worked side by side with a Clovis craftsman. In other words, he was a master emulator, but only a so-so imitator. The same went for every collector and professional archaeologist who examined the points. They focused on shape, which was known to vary considerably, but they didn't know that flake removal exhibited little variation. Perhaps we shouldn't be surprised that Clovis shape and Clovis flake-removal patterns would be driven by different learning and transmission processes. Flaking patterns are a kind of "structural integrity," where key components are more conservative and therefore less likely to change relative to other components. This phenomenon occurs in other aspects of culture as well.

GALTON'S PROBLEM

How much of what animals learn, and how they learn it, is conditioned by genes? Can different groups of the same animal evolve different behaviors, or does being a border collie pretty much lock it into exhibiting the same behaviors, regardless of where it's raised? Or, conversely, are there adaptations that arise in one group that eventually lead its members down different decision-making paths compared to those that other groups take? These questions apply equally to humans. In fact, anthropology and archaeology are littered with the corpses of theories detailing how ideas diffuse between groups, or how one group taught another group, or how two groups independently invented something. These are perfectly reasonable models for social learning, but they have one inherent problem: how do you know that social learning took place at the intergroup level—individuals from one group teaching or learning from another group—as opposed to two unrelated groups arriving at similar solutions to similar problems?

This is called "Galton's Problem," named for Charles Darwin's cousin Francis Galton, and it stems from a meeting of the Royal Anthropological Institute in 1888, where Galton sat listening to a paper being delivered by Edward B. Tylor, whom we mentioned in chapter 1. Recall that Tylor had compiled a series of traits across societies and was arguing that they correlated with his notions that there were stages of social complexity through which all groups progressed. Galton pointed out that that was only one possibility; you could not, on the evidence Tylor had presented, rule out borrowing or common descent for the similarities. To escape Galton's problem requires a handle on how groups are related (or not) to each other.

The same question applies to animal learning. Are there clear-cut cases of different populations of the same species adapting differently in terms of how they learn and make decisions? We know chimpanzees, regardless of location, are members of the same species, so any significant behavioral differences, say, between group A and group B are probably not the product solely of genetics. Almost twenty years ago, Andy Whiten and several other behaviorists, including Jane Goodall, whose work on chimpanzees in Tanzania's Gombe Stream National Park is a model for primate studies, drew on information from long-term studies of behavioral differences among six chimpanzee communities across Africa—four in eastern Africa belonging to one subspecies and two in western Africa belonging to another. They found thirty-nine behavioral variants, including tool use, grooming, and courtship, that were customary or habitual in some communities but absent in others. Significantly, the patterns varied as much between communities associated with each of two subspecies as they did between the subspecies themselves. This finding is further confirmation that chimpanzees, and probably other primates as well, have *cultures*, which we can also label as *traditions*—the maintenance of social contexts in which novel behaviors can be acquired and maintained within a population.

In *Logan's Run*, Box, the robot, was stuck in his program, repeating a behavior useful in the past, but no longer. "Regular storage procedure," repeats Box, "the same as the other food. The other food stopped coming . . . and they came instead. So I store them here. I'm ready. And you're ready. It's my job. To freeze you." Unlike Box, human cultures evolve to meet the demands of new conditions through a mix of learning strategies. And unlike the myriad other animals that learn, humans have a tremendous capacity for cumulative learning. This unique capability to rapidly acquire and retain knowledge—and to disregard knowledge that appears out-dated—is what enables humans to adapt to a vast array of ever-changing environments. Decision-making is like climbing a rugged landscape that is constantly being eroded and uplifted. What works best now might not be what is best later, and even what works now, well, you have to be able to find it in the first place. This is what *fitness landscapes* are all about, which we explore in the next chapter.

DANCING LANDSCAPES AND THE RED QUEEN

As broadband access has come to be seen as a basic human necessity, like water or electricity, the modern economic landscape has changed dramatically from just a generation ago. In Michigan, volunteers with the Detroit Community Technology Project install wireless communications infrastructure in neighborhoods without it, where job seekers otherwise have to find an open computer at crowded public libraries. Being without broadband access is "like fighting without a sword," said a community services director to the *New York Times*. Even where Wi-Fi is freely available, having an older phone is a distinct disadvantage, as almost all job and education applications are online and often require Java or certain downloaded apps. On the modern economic landscape, both access to and skills for using online communications factor into a person's fitness for climbing above the poverty level.

Classical work in biology and ecology helps us understand such a *fitness landscape*—a concept American geneticist Sewall Wright introduced in 1932 to describe how fit an organism is in a particular environment. Each position on the landscape represents a particular genotype, with higher elevations signifying increased fitness and lower elevations decreased or even negative fitness. We can broaden this metaphorical landscape out past genes and use it to examine all kinds of complex adaptive systems that evolve. Within this generic model, a location on the landscape is a solution to a given problem. The elevation of a particular location captures how functional solutions are, with those that are similar in nature being located close together.

To borrow an example from our colleagues at Complexity Labs, consider the different ways of commuting to work in the morning. We have numerous possible strategies, including flying, swimming, driving, or taking the bus. We can create a fitness landscape to represent these strategies and give each option a value based on how well it performs against some measurement of success, such as time or cost. High peaks represent more optimal strategies, lower peaks represent suboptimal strategies, and valleys represent those that don't work at all. The more equal the payoffs are between strategies, the less the difference between the heights of the peaks. Taking a car or a truck to work, for example, might have peaks of the same height and be located next to each other. Very different strategies, such as swimming or flying, would be located farther away and at lower elevations because flying, for example, would cost a fortune in airline fees—a suboptimal commuting strategy (unless you live in Los Angeles and work in Dallas). Walking might be located in between, and the height of fitness peaks could be either quite high (several blocks in a big city) or fairly low (a five-mile hike).

For our prehistoric ancestors, we could imagine even simpler fitness landscapes, say, one that models the Acheulean hand ax—the Pleistocene stone tool that was used for 1.5 million years. Hand-ax shape varied from region to region across Africa, Europe, and western Asia, but not by much. If we modeled the Acheulean ax landscape, we'd have a bunch of short peaks of roughly the same height, and the landscape would look pretty much the same over a very long period of time.

Consider much later Paleolithic hunters, who started making stone spear tips instead of hand axes. The landscape now represents the design of the spear tips, and the heights of the peaks represent how effective the tips are for hunting. As in the figure, three hunters start out on their *adaptive walk* with the same design, so they occupy

Source: Courtesy of Peter A. Bostrum, Lithic Casting Lab

the same spot on the landscape. As they experiment with different design elements, two of them move slowly across the landscape. The third hunter, however, makes a breakthrough improvement in point design and immediately jumps to the top of a nearby peak. His breakthrough is superior to the incremental improvements made by his fellow hunters, and as he continues to make improvements, he jumps from peak to peak on the design landscape, with each jump taking him higher. Meanwhile, experimenting with his own designs, the hunter shown in the middle takes more steps, climbing and jumping along the way, finally landing on the highest peak on the landscape and making his way to the top. The hunter shown at the bottom does well for a while but then takes a path that leads to a lower fitness value before he rights himself and climbs halfway up the slope of the highest peak.

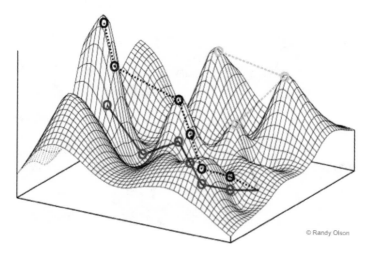

Source: Courtesy of Randy Olson

Now, we can imagine the hunters also sharing their locations—"Hey, I'm over here!"—to help each other navigate across the fitness landscape. In turn, their children would start off on the peaks of their parent(s) and perhaps climb to even higher ones. This represents *cultural knowledge* and the unique human ability for substantially accumulating socially learned information over generations. Human cultural transmission is sometimes characterized in terms of the so-called *ratchet effect*, in which modifications and improvements stay in the population until further changes ratchet things up again.

RUGGED LANDSCAPES

To this point, we've looked at fairly simple landscapes, but let's make things more complicated. This time, instead of stone-tool manufacturers, let's consider a high school student deciding on where she wants to go to college. There are thousands of peaks out there, each comprising multiple factors, including the cost of tuition, geographic location, college ranking, and even the quality of recreational facilities. Although there are multiple peaks, meaning the landscape is *rugged*, it's fairly stable. This means that tuition and housing prices don't fluctuate very much and the prestige of individual colleges and universities remains fairly constant from year to year.

Because our student is savvy—undoubtedly, Buz says, the result of her having taken an excellent introductory economics course in high school—she'll sit back and think of the concepts we talked about in chapter 2: *utility, search goods,* and *experience goods.* Recall that utility refers to the satisfaction you get from buying something or doing something. The *utility function* refers to the fact that when faced with a set of options *and* a limited budget, you decide on the option that leads to the greatest satisfaction. That means that if you really want to go to Yale, and can afford it, you decide on Yale, even though the price might be five times the cost of attending a local university, which you feel is a suboptimal choice. Search goods are those where you already know the payoff and search for the lowest price. For example, our student has researched what an education will be worth thirty years down the line in terms of increased earnings, and she's decided the best place for her is a public institution that's a member of the Association of American Universities—a prestigious self-selecting body of sixty US universities (plus two in Canada) that represent the upper echelon of public and private higher education.

Our student peruses the thirty-four public universities in the group, comparing strength of faculty versus class size versus total cost of attendance. As we said, she's savvy, so she goes to websites such as the *U.S. News and World Report* online information guide to compare universities. Maybe our selective student, even after poring over the vast amount of information on the internet, feels that she doesn't have quite enough information to make a decision that will affect her future fitness, so she decides to pick a university for a year to see if it's the right choice, knowing that she can change if necessary. Here, her decision trends toward an experience good.

Note that we made our student into an ideal case, but most of us fall well short of that. We might know the kind of university we want, and the price we think we can afford, but can we find such a place, given all the choices? Admittedly it's an easier task today than it was a generation ago, given the myriad search engines that are out there, plus websites that allow you to enter your parameters, push a button, and create a list of possibilities. But even then, how do you decide among a long list of options? Those of us who can afford it might go on the old tried-and-true college tour with our parents—a road trip during which we'd visit prospective-student orientations and take college tours—but even with that, there are dozens if not hundreds of other options that we're not exploring. Again, websites help, but can we be sure we're being told the truth? Colleges and universities, especially when their existence is being played out on a highly competitive fitness landscape (see below), will always put their best foot forward, showing pictures of students wearing school colors on their way to class, faculty welcoming them with open arms on the first day of school, and fans cheering in a packed football stadium. We're waiting to see a website that tells it like it really is: "We're okay in science, not so good in the humanities and engineering, but *really* good in music. The dorms seem fine, but maybe you want to go easy on the prepaid meal plan because the food here kind of sucks."

THE LANDSCAPE STARTS TO MOVE

Even though our higher-education landscape has become complex—there are lots of peaks—things aren't changing much across it. What would happen, however, if we allowed for the different variables to constantly change, creating what Stuart Kauffman originally referred to as *dynamic fitness* landscapes and biologist Scott Page refers to as *dancing* landscapes? Here, peaks and valleys undulate over time, even disappearing or suddenly (re)appearing as the result of dramatic changes in the environment. Agents are forced to adapt to the landscape changes, but now their behaviors are continually affected not only by the constantly shifting variables but also by the behaviors of other agents as they try to adapt. How humans respond to the behaviors of others has always been an important variable in cultural evolution, but it assumes primacy on a dancing landscape. As Page describes it, navigating dancing landscapes is like comparing several slot machines in a casino, each having a different payout. The winning strategy here is known as "exploration–exploitation": play one for a while, then another, and when you've found the winning machine, exploit that one. On average, this pays more over time than exploring forever or not exploring at all, assuming the slots stay fixed. But what if the casino changes the payouts on the machines? Now, a player needs to continue to explore at some rate even after finding the better machine. Suppose further that the casino changes the payouts at an ever-increasing rate—so much so that it becomes virtually impossible to keep up. This is a dancing landscape, where one must explore faster and faster in order to stay competitive. This reminds us of Alice in Lewis Carroll's *Through the Looking Glass*, who was told by the Red Queen that "here, you see, it takes all the running you can do, to keep in the same place. If you want to get somewhere else, you must run at least twice as fast as that!"

How does the Red Queen affect our high school student, who is searching the landscape for an optimal college decision for her, and perhaps her parents, in terms of education and affordability? More than one might think because, as we will see, the landscape of American education is dancing faster every day. To start with, although everyone wants the best education that money can buy, even if you have the money it doesn't mean you're going to get accepted at the school you want. And this isn't only for high-end private institutions. Currently in Texas, if you want to attend either of the two public flagship campuses—The University of Texas at Austin or Texas A&M University—you would do well to rank in the top 6 percent of your graduating high school class to have much of a chance. "But wait," our student exclaims. "Last year it was only 8–10 percent!" Yes, it was, but the landscape danced. Apparently no one told her. The websites for the universities certainly didn't. What they say is to get your application in, together with an application fee, your transcript(s), SAT or ACT scores, usually a personal essay, and optional letters of recommendation.

Now, with the landscape changing, our student is not so sure of her decisions and calculations because of an opaqueness to the risks and benefits. Has she considered all the variables? Are the hidden costs associated with getting an education—books and transportation, for example—being figured in? If she intends to live off campus, what will the cost of rent and food be like in two years? If she attends a local college or university, how much cheaper is it to live at home than on campus or in an apartment? (The answer is, a *lot* cheaper.) What is she giving up in terms of college life by living at home? (The answer is, a *lot*.) Perhaps most important, when she's calculating the costs involved, can she be sure of how much debt she'll be racking up? What would happen if federal guaranteed student loans were cut in half? Or if the state in which she intends to go to school cuts its higher-education budget and the school raises its tuition by 25 percent? This has happened more and more frequently in the last decade.

Several years ago, businessman and owner of the NBA Dallas Mavericks Mark Cuban bought the website collegedebt.com. It's a minimalist site, showing only three things: the total amount of auto loans in the United States, the total amount of credit card debt, and a live update of how much college loan debt is held by students. The amount is staggering. In June 2018, the amount of student loan debt stood at $1.6 *trillion*, compared to $1.2 trillion for auto loans and $1 trillion for credit card debt. That amount is still far less than the total mortgage debt in the United States—some $9 trillion—but it's alarming nonetheless.

Our student, together with the hundreds of thousands of other high school students out there in a given year, is not the only agent trying to navigate the highly complex, constantly shifting landscape of higher education. Let's consider what's happening to the colleges and universities. For decades, if not centuries, institutions of higher learning had it pretty easy in terms of occupying, at least for the most part, fairly stable landscapes. They were able to calculate the inputs—the number of students who would attend and the costs associated with offering an education—as well as the outputs—graduation rates, for example. There were, to be sure, downturns—campus riots that destroyed buildings, sanctions leveled against universities by the American Association of University Professors following alleged assaults on academic freedom, and so on—but by and large, the fitness landscape for American higher education, although complex, was stable. And stability meant *predictability*.

However, early in the twenty-first century the landscape began to change dramatically, becoming much more competitive and even cutthroat as the number of high school seniors across the United States dropped significantly and, for many colleges and universities, unexpectedly. Universities in Texas, where people immigrated because of job growth, actually witnessed an increase in applications, but that was an aberration. Universities across the country began offering all kinds of deals in order to attract students, and those were changing on what seemingly was a weekly basis. One trick was to raise tuition but hide it behind the promise of scholarships. This created a false "discount rate": "We're going to cover 39 percent of your tuition with scholarships!! (Oh yeah; we also raised tuition to cover the 'discount,' but we'll keep that a secret.)" Another trick was to raise the cost of residential life—housing plus meals—and then advertise, "The first month is free!"

Another factor that made colleges and universities run faster and faster in terms of decision-making was competition from for-profit institutions. They had been around a long time but rose to become major competitors only when the landscape of higher education changed at the start of the twenty-first century. We've all heard of the University of Phoenix, Capella University, DeVry University, Kaplan University, and other high-profile for-profits, including culinary arts schools such as Le Cordon Bleu, but these represent only the tip of the iceberg. For 2015, the National Center for Education Statistics listed over 3,000 for-profit institutions in the United States.

By mid-decade, with the number of high school seniors on the decline and a new, fierce set of sharks in the water that were promising students faster and cheaper educations, traditional colleges and universities were forced to reevaluate their business models. In the process, they started to view other nonprofits as fair game, looking for any weakness to attack. As we'll see in chapter 7, one major midwestern university became the poster child for bad decisions at critical junctures, and the competition thrived on the fallout. State legislatures and governors added to the landscape complexity by demanding that public colleges and universities not only offer affordable degrees—Rick Perry, the then-governor of Texas, went so far in 2013 as to demand that state institutions offer at least some $10,000 degrees—but do it in disciplines that led to "workforce development." So much for King Lear and Picasso.

Out of desperation, universities started ginning up thousands of online courses to match what the for-profits were doing. They hoped to attract distance-education students who preferred to take classes from home or who lived so far from a traditional campus that it was impractical to attend in person. For some traditional institutions, especially historically black colleges and universities and small private colleges, their landscape changed so fast that they sank financially and either had to close or merge with other institutions. For the students forced to move elsewhere, they suddenly saw their fitness peaks disappear and were dumped back into a valley.

Decisions, decisions, decisions. We've seen the plight of our high school student as she attempts to make an informed choice, and we've seen what colleges and universities are up against on a competitive and ever-changing landscape. The same goes for job seekers and the rapidly changing technological landscape. How, as social scientists, can we make sense of the endless number of decisions that are made and the landscapes on which they're made? What we would like is a tool or set of tools that is not specific to one time in history or prehistory and that helps us organize our thinking in the face of complex and dancing landscapes. As it turns out, there is such a tool. Let's turn the page and see how it works.

6

A MAP IN FOUR PARTS

Imagine a person browsing the electronics section on Amazon or, if you like, a prehistoric forager deciding which stand of trees to visit to gather acorns. In each case, there are many options, and how the person decides will depend on the transparency of how good each option is both intrinsically and socially. *Intrinsic utility* refers to the value something has to you personally, like the calories in those acorns or the useful features of a smartphone. *Social utility* refers to value derived from others liking it or having chosen it. For example, it's intrinsically transparent, at least to most hunter–gatherers who live around oak trees, that acorns will satisfy your hunger. It's socially transparent—from all the people around us who are staring at their phones—that one ought to have a smartphone. It's probably not very intrinsically transparent, however, which model phone to get or which stand of trees produces the best acorns. But we *can* predict that if all the other hunter–gatherers head to one stand of trees, you'll go along with them. That stand has the best *social* utility. Similarly, Amazon may show you the latest iPhone that all your friends have, but it's the social utility as much as the intrinsic utility that leads you to upgrade from your older model.

In both cases, the predictability of choice depends not only on the intrinsic and social utility but also on how transparent those utilities are. Consider something where the intrinsic utility is important and transparent. Say the toilet overflows. You need a plunger, right? So you speed to the hardware store, buy the first one you see on the shelf, speed home, and frantically plunge your toilet. Among all the items in the hardware store—bolts, paint, junction boxes, and Garden Weasels—the toilet plunger, in aisle six, has transparent utility. Among all the hardware in the store, the probability distribution of your choice peaks sharply at that toilet plunger. Likewise, the fitness landscape, representing the utility of all those choices, also peaks at the toilet plunger. In other words, the two landscapes—probability of choice and fitness—are virtually the same: nearly zero for most things in the store except the plunger, which exhibits a sharp peak. The peak does have a few lower peaks associated with it, as there could be a few items that might do the job—some flexible pipe or maybe certain chemicals—but the major peak—the highest-utility option—is clearly the plunger.

Now, let's say you don't go to the hardware store but instead rush to Toilet Barn, which has several aisles of plungers. Or, alternatively, you don't know that a plunger is what unclogs a toilet. In either case, the transparency of the intrinsic options is less. Either you're staring at fifty different plungers trying to decide which one to buy, or you're rummaging through your closets at home for anything that seems like it will do the job. In the case of low transparency, the probability distribution flattens out because utility differences can no longer be easily discerned. At zero transparency, the probability distribution becomes flat, meaning that the choice is effectively random, with equal probability of any particular option being chosen. Even if the probability distribution is flat, the toilet plunger is still the best option. It's just a matter of which one.

This is just for intrinsic utility; if we put social utility back in, then effects are sharpened. With transparent intrinsic utility *and* transparent social utility, people on the optimal peak shout, "Hey; up here!" With transparent social utility but nontransparent intrinsic utility, voices in the fog call out, "Over here!" when in fact they are lost as well, nowhere near the actual optimal fitness peak. Think of a community refusing to get flu shots because "everyone" says that flu shots are dangerous. The peak choice is in one place, and the optimal fitness peak, where everyone is inoculated, is somewhere else.

This is what can happen when social utility is high and intrinsic transparency low. When social influence leads to herding, the most popular option is often not the best one. The probability distribution of choice separates itself from the intrinsic fitness landscape. As it happens, we designed a method of representing this as a two-dimensional map. One dimension plots the magnitude of social influence in the learning process, and the other plots the degree of transparency of costs and payoffs to either social learning or individual learning. These two dimensions are the essence of *discrete-choice* theory with social influence. Discrete choice means that we're looking at choices that are "either/or" as opposed to a continuous choice, such as "how much."

THE MAP

In the simplest of terms, the east–west axis of the map represents learning, and the north–south axis represents the extent to which there is a transparent correspondence between an individual's decision and the consequences—costs and payoffs—of that decision. With respect to learning, the western edge of the map represents completely individual learning and the eastern edge completely

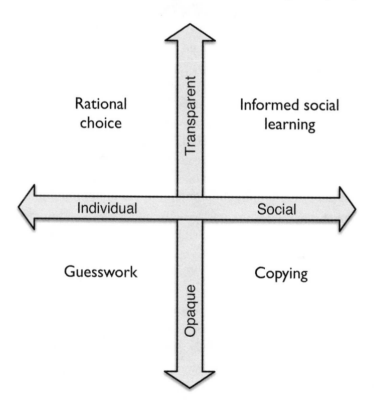

social learning. In between the extremes, the midpoint could represent a population of half individual learners and half social learners or perhaps a situation in which each individual gives equal weight to his or her own experience and those of others.

The north–south dimension represents transparency of choice, from low transparency in the south to high transparency in the north. The farther north we go, the more attuned agents' decisions will be with the landscape. At the extreme northern end, it is clear which decision is optimal and the others less so. As we move south, there are fewer and fewer apparent reasons to prefer one solution over another. At the far south is total indifference or total confusion, where all choices are equally probable. Importantly, even though they have equal probability, choices in the far south could still have very different consequences. There are several reasons for indifference or confusion. For example, people might be poorly informed or just be overwhelmed by too many choices.

We like the map because it distills a vast array of decision scenarios down to the essentials of transparency of choice and social influence. The trade-off, of course, is the simplifying assumptions we must make. First, agents are not assumed to know what is best for them in terms of *long-term* satisfaction, fitness, or even survival. Even rational agents—in the northwest quadrant of the map—who are good at sampling the environment are not omniscient. Neolithic farmers in Europe, for example, were experts at sampling the environment, but they could never have predicted that their descendants would someday be lactose tolerant as a result of their own cheese making. Second, we don't distinguish between learning and decision-making because we're not working at a fine, cognitive scale where it might make a difference. Third, although the map represents a continuous space, we discuss it just in terms of four quadrants: the northwest, northeast, southwest, and southeast. Each quadrant is unique in terms of decision-making and also in terms of the empirical patterns we expect. The patterns would typically be seen in data on the popularity of all the different options over a span of time. Let's explore the quadrants of this map.

NORTHWEST: INDIVIDUAL DECISION-MAKING
WITH TRANSPARENT PAYOFFS

The northwest is where people make decisions individually (independently) based on clear immediate payoffs, such as rushing to the hardware store for a plunger. The rational actor of neoclassical economics lives in the northwest, choosing the option that provides the highest benefit/cost ratio. A bit farther south, but still in the northwest, is where we find decisions made with "bounded rationality," the term first used by behavioral economist Daniel Kahneman, where maximizing the payoffs of a choice is limited by imperfect knowledge in the real world. For the fitness landscape, the northwest is where we find powerful "hill-climbing algorithms" such as reward-driven trial and error and bounded rationality.

In terms of data patterns, the northwest implies that the behavior that yields the best return should become the most popular option and remain so until circumstances change. For example, when Walmart opens its doors on Black Friday, the biggest shopping day of the year, parents make a mad rush—pushing, shoving, and maybe even punching—to the most sought-after kids' toy of the season. In 2017, they would have gone first to aisle four for Fingerlings, the finger puppets that were the hottest toy of the year. After the

Fingerlings were all gone, the mass of parents would turn and head for the second-hottest toy—Hatchimals, in aisle five—until those were all gone. Then they would rush to aisle seven for the DropMix card game, and so on. Behavioral ecologists have a name for this— the ideal-free distribution—where foragers go for the best resource patch first, such as a bend in the river where the salmon run, then if that's not available they go for the next best, which is farther down river, then the next best patch, and so on.

This ideal-free scenario has a simple and predictable pattern of choice popularity over time: one thing sells off, then the next thing, then the next. When its moment comes, the choice follows a basic pattern: a rush of choices the moment it becomes available, followed by a tapering off as fewer of those choices are left to be made, as when the toys are sold off, the fishing spots are all taken, or fewer people remain who haven't already seen the blockbuster movie. The plot of cumulative choices, such as total sales, through time is called an "r-curve" because the cumulative number rises most quickly at first and then levels off, forming an "r."

Another kind of curve is important here, which is the distribution of choices around the mean. Let's say that next to the Fingerlings in aisle four are many other varieties of finger puppets. Fingerlings may be parents' ideal, but the nearby toys represent a distribution around that ideal. If we somehow quantified a set of characteristics describing the toys—size, animal, material, and so on—the distribution of sales would peak around the characteristics of a Fingerling and decline as the characteristics moved away from that ideal. This is actually a method used to study prehistoric stone tools, whose various dimensions are measured and quantified. Around the ideal measurements we get a bell-shaped curve that is high and narrow. Acheulean hand axes, which we discussed in chapter 5, had an unchanging shape for some 1.5 million years, which means that the bell curves of its dimensions remained virtually the same. The reason is that people choose individually based on clear physical constraints of the thing itself; if these constraints change over time, the mean of the normal distribution shifts accordingly.

NORTHEAST: SOCIALLY BASED DECISION-MAKING WITH TRANSPARENT PAYOFFS

As opposed to those in the northwest, behaviors in the northeast spread socially. Once people learn about a new behavior, through any number of social processes, they clearly understand its rationale. In 2007, when people with Nokia phones saw someone using a new iPhone, with its touchscreen and downloadable apps, the reason to get an iPhone was pretty clear (it was awesome). Both the social and intrinsic utility of the iPhone were transparent. In the northeast, better options are made transparent through social interactions, as innovations are discovered and communicated through a population. This takes time, as the idea needs to spread from person to person. The number of adopters through time follows an S-shaped curve, which, unlike the r-curve, starts off slowly, picks up speed as it becomes popular, and then levels off as the majority of people have adopted the idea.

In the northeast, all things being equal, people know who the experts are and can copy their expert choices. We hedge that statement because population size can have a lot to do with being able to identify experts in the first place. As we move south, toward the "equator," the transparency of payoffs begins to blur, and there is more use of unconscious shortcuts that focus on only a portion of the available information. One shortcut is to copy what others are doing, whether it is copying the majority or copying the behaviors of individuals who appear to have the most skill or prestige (see chapter 4). As long as there is some individual learning and decision-making going on within a population—which means anywhere but along the extreme eastern edge of the map—the eventual outcome can be the same as if all learning and decision-making were independent. Along the extreme eastern edge, where there is no independent learning at all to inform the socially learned (imitated) practices in circulation, adaptive potential to an exterior environment is lost. If all you do is copy others, you can become stuck on a suboptimal peak. Efficient communal fishing, for example, requires some boats to try random fishing spots rather than all fishermen visiting the few spots that have been good in the past.

SOUTHEAST: SOCIAL DECISION-MAKING
WITHOUT TRANSPARENT PAYOFFS

The southeast quadrant combines the lack of transparency of payoffs found in the south with the social learning of the east: social learning is high, but transparency is small. The low transparency of choice, like a fog over the landscape, means it's hard to discern the intrinsic payoffs of the choices themselves or even the expertise of people who've made choices. The fog covers the fitness landscape and makes it hard to see the people waving for us to come toward them. The farther south we go, the foggier it gets. In the southeast, you just copy some random person near you in the fog. It's as if each person points to someone else and says, "I'll have what she's having."

The data patterns we expect in the southeast include a popularity distribution that looks like the "long tail" of Amazon book sales, for example: lots and lots of things with few sales and a very few things with a huge number of sales. It's the so-called "80/20" rule, where 20 percent of the items account for 80 percent of the sales, although in reality the number one and two best sellers by themselves might account for half the sales among the thousands of different choices. The other data pattern we expect in the southeast is that popularity is *stochastic*, meaning that the best predictor of popularity at any one moment is popularity in the previous moment, plus a bit of "noise." This means that there is regular change among the most popular items. There is no best option, only a most popular option for the moment, which is continually replaced by other options that drift through the top of the rankings.

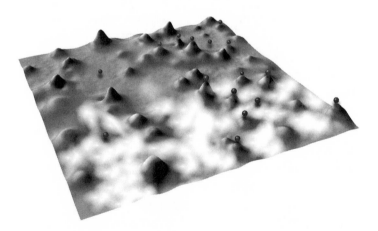

Source: Courtesy of Matthew Boulanger

For this reason, the southeast can be modeled as a process of random copying. Importantly, this does not necessarily imply that agents behave randomly; rather, it says that at the population scale, their biases and individual rationales balance out, making it appear *as if* agents are ignorant of the popularity of a behavior. We draw a distinction between copying *options* at random—which, as we will see, belongs in the southwest quadrant—and copying the *decisions* of other agents. In the southeast, individual learning is at least a small fraction of decision-making, with, say, 5 percent of agents choosing a unique, new variant through individual learning.

SOUTHWEST: INDIVIDUAL DECISION-MAKING
WITHOUT TRANSPARENT PAYOFFS

The southwest quadrant is where you might as well guess because there is no transparency among the options and no opportunity to copy someone else's choice. A good example is encountering many similar options on your own, like a newspaper page filled with mutual funds. Which one will you choose for your retirement plan, when, as we'll talk about in chapter 7, you might have no idea what a plan even looks like? This would be a rare occurrence in small, non-Western societies but a common one in modern capitalist societies, with literally thousands of extremely similar consumer products and numerous sources of information. Here, the popularity of any choice is governed by pure chance. In other words, the southwest is a lottery, and as this lottery is continually repeated, the turnover in popularity of options can be considerable.

Over half a century ago, marketing scientist Andrew Ehrenberg laid out the analytical expectations for the southwest. He showed that when consumers cannot tell the difference among possible choices, the distribution of brand popularity is "short-tailed," which, as the name implies, is quite different from the long-tailed distribution of the southeast. In the southwest, the probability of an option becoming extremely popular—the tail of the distribution—falls off exponentially. Also, when people resort to guesswork, there should be no consistency in the rank order of popularity from one time period to the next. So whereas the one toilet plunger in the hardware store lies in the northwest, choosing from a hundred slightly different plungers at Toilet Barn would be in the southwest—unless you were a plumber and could spot subtle differences.

MOVING AROUND THE MAP

In a piece for the *European Business Review* some years ago, Alex and Mike teamed up with Mark Earls, a market researcher, to suggest that market researchers will want to know where their markets fit on the map. We would now add that really good market researchers will continually update prior knowledge with new observations to make predictions about future events. This is known as *Bayesian inference*. As we put it, four elements—flux, learning, selection, and random events—bring about a new age of models of human behavior. If a market no longer fits in the northwest, there is little value in trying to predict rational and optimal outcomes. If the market plots in the southeast, it is better approached as a matter of insurance or secure investment—coping with unpredictability by maximizing probabilities, minimizing risks, and placing many small bets. Probability distributions, population size, invention rate, interaction networks, and time span become the key parameters in floating with the tides. Marketing becomes less about satisfying the archetypal consumer and more about how many interconnected consumers affect each other's behavior. Old ideas, such as the sanctity of the "brand," have to be recast in terms of this bigger, more anthropological map of human behavior.

Understanding the southeast helps us explain why markets are changing faster than ever and in less predictable ways. Unpredictability is inherent to the southeast. In a controlled experiment, Matt Salganik, Peter Dodds, and Duncan Watts found that people consistently chose the same sorts of music when acting in isolation—the northwest behavior—but when they were allowed to see what songs others were downloading, the behavior became more like in the southeast, meaning it was unpredictable. Despite the fact that we're constantly being overwhelmed with meaningless choices and social influences, individual choice is still the average marketer's default setting. Smart marketers, however, can use this mistaken assumption to their advantage. For example, if a brand becomes popular in the southeast through indiscriminant copying, this luck can be consolidated by moving it to the northwest and concocting any number of post hoc reasons for its success. Or it can be moved to the northeast because of reputation and brand loyalty. Much of what marketers mistakenly call "loyalty," however, remains in the southeast, sustained merely through its own inertia and bound to be ephemeral. Sales data become crucial to being able to distinguish the southeast from the northeast.

These examples of using the map to identify market behaviors represent only the tip of the iceberg in terms of uses. We designed the map to be flexible enough to get people to use it as a basis for interdisciplinary communication and big-picture research, along the way making their own adaptations and modifications. To communicate with a business audience or public policy makers, for example, the north–south axis might be presented as extending from few choices in the north to an overwhelming number in the south. Some psychologists have suggested that the north–south axis might be modified to reflect emotions directly, so that the continuum ranges from purely emotional decision-making (rather than opaque) in the south to purely rational (rather than transparent) in the north. If, in fact, emotions can be used as a proxy for transparency or intensity of choice, then this presents a complementary means of measuring latitude on the map. Others have speculated that the east–west dimension might offer important insights into the dynamics of neural connectivity in small-world properties of brain networks implicated during emotion, social stimuli, social anxiety, and autism. Regardless, for the map to be applicable to decision-making, anywhere from prehistory to the era of big data, we need a minimalist structure that allows for added elements such as emotions collected through surveys or text mining, different concepts of time, and kinship or other cultural constructions, as well as the millennia-worth of material culture in the archaeological record.

What about some of the previous examples we've looked at? Where would they reside on the map? It should be easy to see where our high school student might land as she's choosing a college, depending on her utility function (search criteria) and how identifiable the optimal peaks are. If she has all the information she needs to make the decision on her own, using knowledge gleaned from the internet or perhaps a guidance counselor (guided variation), she would be in the northwest. Maybe, though, she needs to find a few friends who have already been through the process and use them as role models for creating her utility function, which moves her over to the northeast. Or maybe the choices start piling up to the extent that even her friends can't see an optimal peak—or even a suboptimal one—and they start herding toward the southeast corner, looking around and saying, "I'll choose the one they're choosing." Or maybe she's so decision-fatigued that she sighs, tacks a list of colleges on the wall, and throws a dart at it. Our student is now in the southwest.

What about Tom Brady? We would argue that he's squarely in the northwest and won't budge. For him, the optimal peak on the fitness landscape has always been clear, at least during his tenure in professional football. But it wasn't always that way. All young players learn socially, from the players around them and especially from their peers at summer camps. The snap decisions that they're training themselves to make come from a mix of individual and social learning, but over time, there is less and less social learning and more and more social teaching.

What about Brady's team, the New England Patriots? We would argue that the team is also in the northwest because of the success it has had over the past two decades. They've certainly outperformed every other team over that period, so they clearly understand the term "optimality," but it wasn't always that way. Prior to Robert Kraft's buying the team in 1994, it had had an average life since its birth in 1959, appearing in several playoff games, including a Super Bowl (where they were trashed by the Chicago Bears). The Patriots aren't the only team that recognizes optimality peaks, but many of the others appear to occupy parts of the fitness landscape other than in the northwest. As we saw in chapter 3, there is a lot of herding that goes on, where teams follow each other headlong into the southeast.

One type of behavior that we alluded to in chapter 3 but didn't put a label on is *confirmation bias plus weak feedback loops.* Confirmation bias is a form of mistaken choice and/or mistaken belief that requires repeated challenge and strong, immediate feedback to induce rapid learning toward the best choice. Again, this is the foundation of Bayesian thinking, where you continually update prior information using current environmental cues. Weak feedback loops do just the opposite, leading to the dreaded Red Queen effect. Although it is true that confirmation bias and weak feedback loops have nothing to do with social pressures *per se,* there is, as Eli Pariser put it, a "filter bubble," through which your confirmation bias is reinforced by linking you to individuals with similar preferences. Pariser was referring specifically to the internet as the link, but it could just as easily refer to NFL owners and front offices doing business the "traditional" way because everyone else does it that way. Most teams never learn that it pays to be a Bayesian in the NFL.

Let's turn the page and look at a couple more landscapes, neither having much to do with football, except in terms of making money. Robert Kraft and Tom Brady can skip the chapter, but everyone else has to read on.

RISKY BUSINESS

At this point it should be clear that decisions are not locked into specific regions of the map but can move around, depending on time and context. For example, you might be in the southwest because you're on your own and you can't distinguish risks from benefits. Tomorrow, though, you might talk with knowledgeable friends and bone up on the issue, at which point you're beginning to move northward, bit by bit. Or maybe you think long and hard about something and suddenly remember that you've seen this problem before. You then pull it out of long-term memory and into working memory, which moves you toward the northwest. These are the stories with happy endings, but what about those that might not end so well? Let's look at two examples.

TAKING STOCK(S) OF RETIREMENT

Our first example starts out in the northeast, with Alex's first day at his new university job. He actually started out in the southwest, not knowing much, if anything, about the new job, but he started moving into the northeast, absorbing everything the experts told him at the new-employee orientation—how to sign on to the computer system, where to catch a campus bus, and where to buy football tickets. One session was dedicated to health-and-retirement benefits, where employees were introduced to various retirement-plan options as well as to several companies that managed the options. If you consider all the possible permutations of just three aspects of the decisions that an employee faces—different companies, multiplied by the dozens of different plans they offer, multiplied by the number of different levels of financial contribution that are possible—it begins to run into thousands of possible solutions. Also, this is a future-oriented decision, with countless unknowns that will affect one's potential well-being decades into the future. Despite starting out in the northeast with a sense of optimism, Alex is now so thoroughly confused that he quickly slides back to the southwest.

If you're content with throwing a dart at the open pages of the *Wall Street Journal* as a means of making decisions, you're happy in the southwest. But considering his future, Alex would rather be farther north, either in the northwest, inheriting optimal behavior from his ancestors through guided variation, or back in the northeast, understanding from the experts what his options really are. In terms of future planning, the southwest can be a precarious place in which to make decisions, given that the supremely important evolutionary variable is reproductive success. Remember that decisions about such things as retirement options affect not only your future but those of your children and grandchildren. Choose the best retirement plan out of the thousands of options—you won't know for decades—and maybe your grandkids can each have a trust fund and afford four years at an Ivy League school. That, together with the network contacts they make there, could change the fitness of your whole descendent lineage.

It's no accident, for example, that President George W. Bush graduated from Yale, as had both his father, President George H. W. Bush, and his grandfather, Prescott Bush. Legacies, both biological and cultural, are the essence of reproductive success. The children of the late Robert Kardashian, one of O. J. Simpson's defense lawyers, have made a fortune out of "being famous for being famous," as British journalist Malcolm Muggeridge put it, just by having a

Source: Courtesy of S. Buckley, Shutterstock

father thrust into the limelight at exactly the right time. Of course, from an evolutionary standpoint, publicity can definitely enhance fitness. Tallulah Bankhead, the renowned stage actress of the forties and fifties, knew all about fitness, once saying, "I don't care what they say as long as they talk about me."

Let's go back to Alex's employee orientation. Aiming for the northeast, he decided to call in the experts, the university's contracted financial advisors, for a personal consultation. He happily let them choose his retirement plans, but then they asked how he wanted to invest the funds in each plan. The choices included dozens of company-managed funds with names like "balanced midcap funds" and "world growth and aggressive excellence funds," each comprising wide varieties of stocks, bonds, and derivatives. The self-evaluation questionnaire that the advisors offered Alex— "Would you rather have an 85 percent chance of getting a 10 percent annual return, or a 15 percent chance of losing 5 percent in certain years?"—did not help. He was still stuck in the southwest.

Alex was on an extremely rugged, and dancing, fitness landscape, with peaks and deep valleys side by side, with his financial wellbeing resting on an hour-long appointment. In other words, aiming for the northeast by seeking expert advice, Alex nevertheless remained in the southwest, having to make quick decisions among countless options with nearly zero transparency. With no idea which choices were best for his grandkids, he let the advisors choose for him, signed his name several times and initialed under each section of fine print, and let the advisors hurry on to their next meeting. This decision journey ended in the southwest, where fog obscures the peaks of optimality. Utility function? Search goods? Not visible. And remember, the "experts" one uses to try to get to the northeast are salespeople, and they live on a different fitness landscape—one based on sales and not necessarily on one's financial well-being.

Is it any different for active stock traders? Do they have access to transparency, and hence optimality, that others don't? We all hear stories of traders who make fortunes, many of them "common folks" like us. We don't doubt that some people exhibit an uncanny ability to pick winners, but we know they are few and far between. One recent survey, for example, noted that 99 percent of day traders eventually lose all the money they invest. No doubt Warren Buffett is an exception, and if you want to follow him and develop the same kind of portfolio he has, that's fine, but he's not bulletproof, and he knows it. Buffett bought Berkshire Hathaway, a New England textile manufacturer, in 1964, but it hemorrhaged money and finally closed. He later called it his dumbest investment. It did, however, provide him with a platform, of the same name, from which to buy other companies. Berkshire Hathaway has beaten the market over the long run by investing in relatively low-risk stocks the market underprices, and investors have reaped the profits. An investor who bought one share of Berkshire Hathaway at just over $11 when Buffett took control, and kept it, would have seen its value hit above $300,000 in early 2018, an annual return of 21 percent, which is far above what the markets have done.

Fine, we say, let Buffett be the expert that we follow in the northeast, where there is transparent social learning. But, as we've seen, transparency doesn't always equal success, whether you're trying to reproduce a Clovis point or Warren Buffett's success. We doubt few people really can imitate Buffett, even the tens of thousands who crowd the annual Berkshire Hathaway shareholder meeting the first weekend of May in Omaha, Nebraska, to participate in lively discussions and hear from Buffett and his management team. We're betting some of them are pretty good emulators—they're making money—but nowhere near as good imitators. They don't have hordes of researchers at their disposal, nor do they have the time to invest in the research themselves, but they can learn at least some basics that might help them scale a fitness peak or two. A better strategy would be to invest in Berkshire Hathaway and let Buffett and his team do all the work. But even here, Buffett is smarter, and more honest, than most fund managers and CEOs. "I don't want anybody buying Berkshire thinking that they can make a lot of fast money," Buffett told biographer Alice Schroeder. "They're not going to do it, in the first place. And some of them will blame themselves, and some of them will blame me. They'll all be disappointed. I don't want disappointed people. The idea of giving people crazy expectations has terrified me from the moment I started selling stocks." That's one reason his class-A shares sell for over $300,000: it keeps uninformed people out of the market and protects their money. Buffett's advice to the average investor? Invest in index funds. Buffett has been called the "Oracle of Omaha," but we'd call him the "King of the Northeast."

Buffet is an excellent role model for investors because in addition to being smart, he learns socially by paying attention to the advice given him by the team he's assembled. Of course, you might be so sure of yourself that you don't even begin to think that you need advice about risks and benefits—that they are so transparent that you can easily top the highest peaks of optimality without help. If you really *do* know everything, we'll gladly put you way up in the northwest corner, but we have to stop and ask ourselves if perhaps you just *think* you do. If you're wrong, what might the consequences be, for both you and everyone else? Let's keep reading and find out how such a tiny error in self-perception can have cataclysmic results and turn a fitness landscape into a sea of chaos.

I NEED SOME MUSCLE OVER HERE!

This particular decision pathway involves a series of incidents that occurred at the University of Missouri in 2015–2016 while Mike was serving as dean of the college of arts and science. Founded in 1839 in Columbia, the University of Missouri is the oldest public university west of the Mississippi River. It was modeled after Thomas Jefferson's masterpiece, the University of Virginia, with stately red-brick buildings surrounding a large grassy quad, a focus on an arts and sciences curriculum, and a strong commitment to both its students and the state's citizens. It was given land-grant status in 1870 under the Morrill Act of 1862, and in 1908 it joined the elite group of major research universities we mentioned in chapter 5, the Association of American Universities. The flagship Columbia campus was eventually joined by three other schools to form the University of Missouri System. Each campus is headed by a chancellor, who reports to the system president.

Public universities like Missouri depend on both tuition/fee revenue and state appropriations to survive, and each state plays things a bit differently. Some provide little revenue for their public colleges and universities, making them depend more on tuition and fees. Here, the landscape is rugged but still fairly predictable, as long as the number of students increases or at least stays steady. We saw in chapter 5, though, that all hell can break loose when the number of students declines, either through a demographic downturn or fierce competition from other institutions (or both). At that point, decisions made by recruitment officers, admissions directors, financial-aid officers, and marketing strategists become all the more important. Most of the time, though, regardless of the chaotic nature of the higher-education landscape, a dean's job stays pretty much the same. Most deans reside somewhere in the northwest, where there are fairly well-understood risks and benefits. This doesn't mean that deans are always paying attention, but it's a good bet that failure is due to hubris, neglect, or a dozen other failings and not to opaqueness.

Following the US financial crisis of 2007–2008, the University of Missouri was still able to increase enrollment because of a very good football team, new dormitories, a state-of-the-art recreation center, and a world-class journalism school. All that began to change in February 2014 with the appointment of a new campus chancellor, who came from Texas A&M and loved to say, "This is not my first rodeo; I know how to do this." As with many who use that cliché, that wasn't exactly true. Although no one knew it at the time, an incident that was mishandled by university personnel lit a slow-burning fuse that eventually ended in disaster. That incident was the August 2014 shooting death of Michael Brown in Ferguson, Missouri, a suburb of St. Louis about two hours east of Columbia. Understandably, many of the African American students on campus wanted to talk about safety, civil rights, and equity. Various forums were set up, but the students soon realized that they were being patronized and that their concerns were not being taken seriously. This seemed to be a deliberate decision: "Let the students air concerns, but do not engage in responding. After a while, things will quiet down."

They did for a while, but the fuse continued to burn. Things exploded a year later, when graduate assistants, the lifeblood of any research university, woke up on a Saturday morning in August 2015 to find out their tuition waivers and health-insurance subsidies were being cut. After a storm of protest from students and faculty, the chancellor eventually restored the tuition waivers and health benefits for another year, but he did nothing to restore affordable housing and childcare, which had been taken away earlier that year. Graduate students threatened to unionize, protests continued, and things got worse. Black students jumped on board and formed a protest group, "Concerned Student 1950," referring to the first year the university admitted black students. They attempted to disrupt the fall 2015 homecoming parade in October to get attention, but they mistook the system president's car for the chancellor's car. When the president didn't stop and talk to them—a bad decision, he later admitted—the students started calling for his resignation. The chancellor, meanwhile, had only a brief respite from the chaos swirling around him. He hadn't foreseen the anger that was building among the deans, who were outraged that in September the chancellor had called in the dean of the medical school one Monday morning, less than a year after hiring him, and told the dean to sign a letter of resignation or he'd fire him. Unfortunately, in the heat of chaos, adrenaline kicks in, and the perception of long-term payoffs is discounted by payoffs of the moment. The dean signed the letter.

Mike had made his mind up early on that the chancellor had to go before he destroyed the university. He made the decision on his own—in the northwest—not knowing how the other deans would respond. Most were younger and had promising careers, and several had young children. The risks involved with trying to take down a university chancellor are actually quite simple: if you fail, you're toast. In Missouri, only the university president, in consultation with the governing Board of Curators, can fire a chancellor. Although the problems on campus were obvious to them, to let a chancellor go after less than two years would publicly signal their mistake in hiring him in the first place. One by one, the other deans became aware of what was happening, and within a few weeks all nine sitting deans were on board. All of them were fully aware of the risks, and they put their careers on the line. No southern half of the map for them.

Meanwhile, things on campus kept getting worse. On November 8, the black football players announced that they had decided to boycott the upcoming game against Brigham Young University, and their teammates and coaches stood with them. This angered thousands of Missouri fans. In addition, a black graduate student had recently declared he was on a hunger strike until death, if that's what it took to get the president—not the chancellor, under whose watch all the mess was occurring—to resign. Black students started organizing class walkouts and marches, and they took to camping out on one of the quads.

Adding to the chaos on the night of November 11, 2015, the hashtag #PrayforMizzou began trending on Twitter, warning residents that the KKK was in town and had joined the local police to hunt down black students. One user included the picture of a severely bruised black child, claiming it was his little brother. It wasn't; it turned out to be a year-old picture from Ohio. Other tweets claimed that there were widespread shootings, stabbings, and cross burnings. Even the student body president, a young black man, got in on the act, posting on Facebook, "Students please take precaution. Stay away from the windows in residence halls. The KKK has been confirmed to be sighted on campus. I'm working with the [campus police], the state trooper and the National Guard." He later rescinded the post, which was false, but the damage had already been done.

These claims should have been seen as patently ludicrous, but there were hundreds of people—white and black—who believed them. This behavior is in the far southeast corner of the map, where we find pure herding. Meanwhile, a female faculty member in Mike's college, who was one of a large group of people cordoning off the black-student camp on the quad, was caught on camera shoving a student reporter and yelling, "I need some muscle over here!" in reference to keeping reporters at bay. That scene was viewed by tens of millions on television the next evening, which led to thousands

Source: Courtesy of Mark Schierbecker, YouTube

of e-mails and tweets, most wanting her head on a stake—another example of a rush to the southeast.

To jump to the end of the story, the deans had confronted the chancellor in a meeting in the president's office in mid-October and one by one told him they wanted him gone. On November 9, they did what a reporter for the *Chronicle of Higher Education*, Jack Stripling, labeled as throwing a Hail Mary pass. They fired off a letter to the board and the president asking for the chancellor's immediate removal, saying he had failed as a leader and had created "a toxic environment through threat, fear and intimidation." The letter was leaked to the press later that morning, and as Stripling put it, the deans "were all in." Here, a collective decision affected an individual's fitness. By late that afternoon, the chancellor was no longer chancellor.

Was that the end of the story? Not by a long shot. After the chancellor's removal, the Missouri legislature collectively decided to punish the university for allowing all the chaos to happen in the first place. Then, parents and students of all persuasions began to vote with their feet. The fall 2016 enrollment was stunning: 2,000 fewer students than in fall 2015, followed by another 2,000-student decline the next year. The newly hired vice provost for enrollment noted that the university had studied the causes for the dramatic drop and reached the conclusion that "the vast majority of our undergraduate enrollment concerns are closely tied to our public perception issues throughout the state and throughout the country." Really? We hope the university didn't spend a whole lot of time and money to reach *that* conclusion. The enormous loss of revenue created a financial crisis that will hamstring the university for years. To our point, the entire mess started with crucial decisions being made, or driven by, actions in the southwest quadrant of the map.

As a postscript, a sense of normalcy slowly began to return with the appointment of a well-liked administrator as interim chancellor—someone who had his head in the northwest. The dean of the medical school was reinstated—much to the delight of the other deans—and the football coach retired "for health reasons." You just have to wonder, though, what would've happened if, when confronted by his players about the planned boycott of the upcoming football game, the coach had said something like, "Guys, I love each and every one of you like a son, and I respect your decision not to play. But I want you to know that when you walk out that door, you need to lay your scholarships on the table because I'm going to give them to guys who want to play Saturday night in Kansas City. Good luck to you." His failure to make that decision cost the university dearly in terms of support from alumni, students, and the legislature. Finally, it turned out that the hysteria caused by the tweets and retweets that fateful November 2015 night—the ones that said the KKK and neo-Nazis were in Columbia—was the product of none other than Russian hackers. Should we be surprised? No. Should we be alarmed that people are allowing themselves to be manipulated by hackers and bots instead of making independent decisions? Yes. Let's turn the page and see how bad it can get.

LIFE IN THE SOUTHEAST

At the aggregate level of decision-making—admittedly painting with a fairly broad brush—hominin evolution may have witnessed a clockwise progression from individual learning in the northwest, to the group traditions of the northeast with the development of the social brain, and then to the south, particularly to the southeast, as information and interconnected population sizes increased exponentially through time. If we consider the smaller societies of human prehistory, crucial resource-allocation decisions would plot in the northern half of the map, with more specific behaviors ranging between the northwest and the northeast. The same should apply to health decisions. Joe Henrich and James Broesch asked Yasawa Islanders of the South Pacific, "Whom would you go to for advice if you had a question about using a plant as a medicine?" Several Yasawans emerged as perceived experts and were twenty-five times more likely than others to be sought out for advice on medicinal plants.

In today's large, interconnected world, however, we might find ourselves asking, "Who needs role models and experts when everyone can follow trends, especially those that appear to be hot?" As we saw in chapter 6, however, those trends tend to be short-lived, and there's a constant churn of alternatives. It becomes more and more difficult for learning processes to discover which options are in fact even marginally better than others. This, in turn, pushes decision-making southward and paradoxically could mean that modern diverse consumer economies might be less efficient test tubes for the testing and winnowing of life-improving technologies and medicines than societies were in the past.

Things, as we saw in chapter 7, can turn out badly when we live in the southwest, but what about the southeast? How does that affect our fitness? Well, for one thing, if we go too far to the southeast, the distributed mind, which represents a huge fitness benefit when minds are thinking *individually*, begins to corrode, so much so that behavior becomes nothing but herding. At that point, the wisdom-of-crowds effect is lost. In economies replete with online communication and a constant barrage of information, crucial human decision-making is becoming more herd-like in contexts such as voting, forming opinions about climate change, and finances. Another area in which this is occurring is one in which the three of us are involved on a daily basis: academic publishing. Let's take a look and see how decision-making related to the conduct of research and the dissemination of knowledge have moved around the map and are now heading to the southeast.

PAY FOR PLAY

Several years ago, Mike and his wife, Gloria, were in Seoul to discuss student and faculty exchanges between the University of Missouri and a few Korean universities. During one conversation, the president of a prestigious private university asked Mike to name what in his opinion were the top three scientific journals in the world. The first two were easy—*Science* and *Nature*—and Mike thought for a minute and decided on *Cell* as the third. "Yes," the president responded, pleased with the choices. "We refer to them as *"SNiCk."* He continued, "How much do you pay your researchers at the University of Missouri for publishing in one of those journals?" Mike demurred, as US universities do not pay bounties, and asked the president if *his* university paid and, if so, how much. The president responded, "$25,000." Mike was sure the president meant 25,000 Korean won, or about $25, but the president assured him that his English was much better than Mike's Korean. The president said he had to do this to get his faculty to begin to move out of a parochial mind-set and onto the world scientific stage. Knowing the next university on Mike's tour, the president said to ask that institution's president what *his* policy was. The answer, it later turned out, was a staggering $100,000 per article. The president proudly stated that he had written two such checks that year. Mike told Gloria they were immediately moving to South Korea.

An incentive like this is bound to change the fitness landscape, but the change is going to be slow. Despite the lure of a huge check, the odds of publishing in *Science*, *Nature*, and *Cell* are exceedingly small, made even smaller when there is no established culture of publishing in high-visibility, high-impact journals. The alternative for the majority of researchers around the world, including the United States, is to take advantage of the tremendous increase in the number of academic journals that have hit the market over the past few years. And we do mean *market*. Journal publishing worldwide produces annual revenues of over $10 billion. Literally millions of papers are published every year in the pages of some 30,000 allegedly peer-reviewed journals, and this doesn't even begin to count those that are not peer-reviewed. More on that in a minute.

Think of the difference between now and 1665, when the Royal Society of London, commissioned by King Charles II and chaired by Bishop John Wilkins, published the first issue of its *Philosophical Transactions*. Members of the seventeenth-century Royal Society included architect and astronomer Christopher Wren; the founder of modern chemistry, Robert Boyle; physicist Robert Hooke; and Isaac Newton. The society was solidly in the northeast, with experts working alongside experts to create the foundations of chemistry, biology, physics, philosophy, and the Enlightenment—the "wisdom of groups" comprising free-thinking individuals. As peers without peers, these experts were able to interact with each other and select the best ideas through the idealized process of science, which is the independent testability of hypotheses with clear, widespread dissemination of scientific results. This is what philosopher Philip Kitcher described as unification, fecundity, and testability, which translates into the "wisdom of groups."

It used to be that an academic journal came out quarterly. A few came out more frequently, but even then, you could manage to keep up with the flow of new information. Now, even seasoned researchers can't keep up. The change agent, of course, has been the internet. So many articles are now published online that the paper editions are years behind. Some journals have even dropped the idea of volume numbers altogether and are simply indexing an article by its digital object identifier, which is a number string unique to that article. Open-access, peer-reviewed "megajournals," such as *PLOS ONE, Palgrave Communications,* and *Scientific Reports,* publish thousands of articles a year, charging authors a fee of $1,000 or more per article. With this kind of revenue generation, university presses have jumped in as well. For example, the University of California Press launched *Collabra* in 2011, with an article fee of $875. The publishing landscape also contains thousands of start-up journals, many carrying reputable-sounding titles but which are nothing but pay-for-play rags. Academics are spammed on a daily basis with invitations to publish in a brand-new journal. The email usually starts out something like this:

> Dear esteemed MJ Obrien:
> We are soliciting an article from you for our new journal,
> *Advances in World Urology,* given our reading of your article
> "The Paleoindian Colonization of North America." It could
> be a new paper or one published previously. It can be long
> or short. And as a contributor to this special edition, you will
> have your publication fee waived.

Wow; what a deal. No $1,500 publication fee *and* the opportunity to publish in a journal that has no connection to your expertise. Anyone would jump at the chance, even if the journal editor can't spell your last name correctly. Unfortunately, plenty of people *do* jump. As more and more researchers enter the academic arena worldwide, the number of journals that do not solicit peer review of their articles will only increase, and the pay-to-play aspect of academic publishing will become the mainstay.

The Korean university presidents knew that where one publishes is the most important component of someone's intellectual fitness. Academics (hopefully) are judged more on the quality of their work than on the quantity of publications they have. At reputable universities, faculty committees that are reviewing their peers' work shouldn't be fooled by low-quality, pay-for-play journals, especially when they have a battery of tools at their disposal, including those that list how many times a particular article has been cited—and where—and what a journal's impact factor is. That means how many times articles in a journal get cited. Journal-impact factors are—or should be—important inputs into decisions about where to publish one's work.

As researchers are deluged with articles, even the most experienced are rapidly losing the capacity to even begin to evaluate all the literature that might be relevant and of sufficient quality. There are a few shortcuts, though they have their downsides. One is to read only *SNiCk* and *SNiCk*-like journals, which is a move to the northeast quadrant, in that you consider the editors of those top journals to be experts and to accept papers only from other experts. Then again, there are a lot of quality journals out there—maybe not in the top tier but close—that you're passing up. Another shortcut is to follow the work of just your friends and colleagues, though Buz and his colleague Steven Durlauf showed twenty years ago that this can lead to academic "cartels," the members of which read and cite only each other's work, oblivious of much of the relevant research that goes on outside their group. In social-learning terms, they become scroungers on the fitness landscape rather than dividing their efforts between scrounging and producing.

Another option, which is becoming increasingly widespread, is to train a computer to evaluate the science for you. As the University of Chicago's James Evans and Jacob Foster noted, a computer "can rapidly access quantitative and relational information about authors, terms, and institutions" and compare it to "millions of articles and an increasing pool of digitized books." This kind of data scraping is now a common occurrence, but even it has limitations, especially with respect to evaluating the quality of the terabytes of research data. Elsevier, a major journal publisher, has a tool called "SciVal," which analyzes citation data from over 9,000 research institutions to map the competitive strengths of research in 230 regions and countries. Academics are adapting to this landscape by making themselves more discoverable. Over a million scholars now have an ORCID ID, that is, an identifier for a system created by a nonprofit in 2012 to serve as a registry for individual researchers and to connect them to an application programming interface so that different systems can share information about researchers. This is just the beginning, as the coevolution of computer algorithms reading papers, and the meta-data associated with those papers to make them more readable by computer, could, for better or worse, lead to fully computerized, hypothesis-driven science.

WE'RE ALL SCIENTISTS NOW

If it sounds like academic publishing has become an electronic marketplace, it's because it has. It works the other way, too. Three and a half centuries after the Enlightenment, we make literally hundreds of decisions every day, collecting and evaluating data, often on completely new situations or challenges. It used to be you were a potato farmer, banjo player, blacksmith, or textile weaver because one of your parents taught you the trade from a young age. Now, because of instant access to data and trends, we're seemingly all scientists. It can be downright challenging to know who the experts are. The forces of change no longer emanate predictably from the Royal Society. As we saw in chapter 7, decisions can light fuses that are so small as to be seemingly inconsequential and yet are tipping points for events that end up cascading through a population. The fitness landscapes are not only rugged but also ever changing in terms of risks and benefits. Here, optimality is difficult to spot. The concepts of expertise and rational choice seem all but laughable in the era of social media, where false news seems to be more the norm than the exception.

The lifeblood of false news is social media, especially Facebook and Twitter. In terms of the map, each time someone tweets something on his or her own, we may consider it an individual learning event, which puts it in the west. When someone retweets it, it's a copying event, which is in the east. If someone tweets his or her own individual discovery, something discovered through creativity, research, observation, or experiment, then it's in the northwest. Whereas a true "Eureka!" discovery would be an individual, transparent decision in the northwest, someone tweeting random garbage—just trying to stir things up—maps in the southwest. If people are retweeting things just because others are tweeting about the same thing, we would place it in the southeast—a form of random copying that can have serious consequences.

But what about the northeast, which contains transparent social learning? Here, the most important variable is *whom* we are copying, not necessarily what, or even whether it is true. Not only does prestige matter in terms of whether we "believe" the message, group identity may also be as important as "truth." If we identify with a message, we'll probably retweet it. Whether we believe the rumor to be true might be close to irrelevant. For the fecundity of rumor (meme) itself, all that matters is whether we pass it on. So the northeast, where we expect well-informed social learning, could indeed contain a lot of false messages, which nevertheless ring "true" in terms of the group identity of those sharing it. The social affiliation of the message is often quite transparent, even if the content message itself is false—like wearing a Patriots jersey even though your physique tells the world you probably never played football and certainly not for New England.

As destructive as partisanship might be to the common good, there is a transparent social logic to following your tribe, which would map in the northeast. Not surprising, a study of following and retweeting behavior on Twitter indicates that online polarization has increased by about 20 percent since 2009. Online social networks are segregated to a point where each faction selects its false news of choice. This tendency of like to affiliate with like is known as *homophily*, which can, in turn, lead to the sorting of information. Yet social media has only continued a partisanship that has been growing since the mid-twentieth century. Bipartisan agreement on legislative decisions declined steadily in the US House of Representatives from 1949 to 2012, Clio Andris of Penn State and colleagues found. Over those sixty-plus years, the networks of red and blue—representing who voted with whom on legislation—evolved from a tangled web of cooperation after World War II to two separate networks—one red, one blue—linked only by a few representatives committed to cooperating across party lines. Political partisanship shows no sign of slowing down or reversing course, Andris and colleagues concluded.

Are we confined to tribalism of the northeast? Well, as behavioral economist Daniel Kahneman put it, "[T]hinking is to humans as swimming is to cats; they can do it but they'd prefer not to." Imagine that someone sees false news on Twitter, resists the impulse of group affiliation, and instead fact-checks it and tweets that the rumor is false. We are moving back toward the northwest, but maybe not for long. Because the fact-checked message is boring and does not stoke the fires of online tribal warfare, it may go nowhere. Or, if it serves as an "in your face!" argument, it might set off a cascade of retweeting by whichever political side it serves. If this happens, it may well be transformed by both sides, one exaggerating the argument and the other hyperbolizing the counterargument, and so on. Novel and disgusting elements of the story will be retained and/or amplified as the message is passed on, as we saw in chapter 7 with respect to the University of Missouri.

Research by MIT's Sinan Aral and colleagues revealed how true and false news spreads differently online, in ways that reflect just what we expect from our map. This includes the distributions characterizing how far and how fast rumors spread (both higher for false news) as well as the sentiments of the stories themselves—false news tends to be more surprising, disgusting, and scary. Each spread event on Twitter is a *rumor cascade*, where a user makes an assertion about a topic in a tweet and others propagate it by retweeting it. The size of the cascade can be small or large. If a rumor is tweeted by ten people separately, but not retweeted, it would have ten cascades, each of size one. If another rumor is independently tweeted by two people, and one is retweeted 150 times and the other retweeted 2,000 times, then there are two cascades of the rumor, each of a different size.

Aral and colleagues observed 126,000 rumor cascades on Twitter between 2006 and 2017 that had already been fact-checked by organizations such as factcheck.org and where at least 95 percent of the fact-checkers agreed on whether the rumor itself was true or false. They measured three properties for each cascade. The *size* of the cascade was the total number of people involved in retweeting a tweet. The *depth* of a cascade measured how many hops back the last person to receive the message would need to get back to the original tweet—like the length of a transmission chain. *Breadth* measured the number of different chains running at any one time. Breadth and depth describe the size of the cascade in the way branches describe the size of a tree. Breadth is like how many leaves there are, and depth is like how many branches there are from a leaf to the trunk. Another measure, which they called *structural virality*, distinguished between those messages that spread in *r*-curve fashion, by means of a single broadcast or famous individual, and those that diffused in S-curve fashion, being copied along multiple transmission chains.

The MIT findings fit what we'd expect from our map, where the distribution of cascade size—the same was true for depth and breadth—was more short-tailed for the true information and more long-tailed for the false information. This pattern maps true information in the west and false information in the east, which makes sense because true information is more likely to be individually considered. In fact, the true information took longer on average to cascade from user to user than the false rumors. Doing some critical thinking about information is more time-consuming and costly than taking the shortcut of just copying your peers. In other words, true information being shared has elements of individual learning mixed in with the social aspect of sharing it and should be more short-tailed in the distribution. False rumors, not surprisingly, have a long-tailed distribution, just as we would expect in the east.

How far north or south were these rumor cascades? We'd expect, of course, the true information to be toward the north and the false information toward the south. As mentioned above, the MIT team found false rumors spread farther and faster and tended to be more surprising and novel, as well as more disgusting and scary, than true information. True stories were more likely to be sad or happy and inspire trust. Again, this is consistent with people taking more time to reflect on the true information and consider the payoffs more transparently than with the false information, which is handled with the kind of herd responses we rely on in scary or surprising situations. Believing false news might make us feel scared, but in some ways, this "scariness" has been building for a long time. Fear-related words, for example, have been on the rise in English-language books since at least the 1980s, unlike most other emotions, which have decreased since the early twentieth century. Why? Perhaps it has something to do with the dissolution of kin groups and proliferation of decisions that people had never encountered before, from the monumental to the mundane. This must be upsetting for a species that evolved living in small groups of well-known kin, making decisions according to adaptive cultural recipes that had been handed down through countless generations.

DECISION FATIGUE

We live in an era when Amazon has over half a *billion* products for sale. That incredible number of options is the reason why Liberty

Media chairman John Malone referred to the company as a "death star" that's moving into striking range of every industry on Earth. And we once thought of Amazon as a quaint online bookstore. Oxford's Eric Beinhocker describes the explosion in modern Western human choice as a "hundred million-fold, or eight orders of magnitude difference in the complexity and diversity" from what our hunter–gatherer ancestors witnessed 10,000 years ago. It might seem strange to discuss shopping on Amazon along with other decisions we've discussed in this book—choosing a jury, where a young woman should go to college, how to invest both for one's retirement and for that of one's children, and even what quarterback to draft—but we think it makes a strong point in terms of how seemingly small and perhaps insignificant decisions are consuming our brain power. The University of Florida's Aner Sela and his University of Pennsylvania colleague Jonah Berger put it this way: "People often find themselves mired in seemingly trivial decisions. We agonize over what toothbrush to buy, struggle with what flight to purchase, and labor over which shade of white to paint the kitchen. While common wisdom and much research suggest that people should deliberate harder the more important the decision, why do people sometimes get stuck in seemingly minor choices?" Sela and Berger suggest that metacognitive inference is behind this "decision quicksand." Their premise is that people use the subjective difficulty they experience while making a decision as a cue to how much more time and effort to spend on it. We expect that more important decisions are more difficult to make, being that they involve higher risks, and as a result we expect decisions about seemingly more trivial matters to be easier because of the lower risks involved in making a bad decision.

What happens, though, when a decision suddenly and unexpectedly feels difficult—perhaps the result of too many choices, information overload, or seemingly conflicting risks and payoffs? Sela and Berger propose that people might draw the reverse inference that the decision is important and deserving of additional attention. This, in turn, increases the amount of time people use in reaching a decision. Because the tendency to associate the importance of a decision with decision difficulty is so strong, we sometimes artificially complicate important decisions that "feel" too easy so that we can adopt an air of confidence that we've conducted appropriate due diligence. Let's go down to the toothpaste aisle at Walmart and spend a few minutes looking at the people around us making decisions about which brand to buy. They won't spend as much time as they would if they were buying a house or deciding where to go to college, but we'll bet that we notice at least one or two people exhibiting a mild form of decision quicksand. If they throw up their hands and just grab a tube, they're in the southwest. If they look around at various shopping carts and go with the most popular brand, they're in the southeast.

WHAT ABOUT THE FUTURE?

Decision fatigue over picking out a toothpaste brand is one thing, but where might we be headed with respect to more serious issues such as global warming, the validity of news, or foreign meddling in American life, science, and politics? In our opinion, we are moving rapidly to the extreme southeast on these and other significant issues. Despite an enormous wealth of information on global warming, a significant percentage of Americans pooh-pooh the idea, blaming left-leaning scientists and news sources for the scare, not even bothering to try to understand the science behind the claims. Of course, for their part, scientists don't always make clear the difference between global warming and the impact of humans in the warming, which leaves them open to misinterpretation.

Foreign meddling is particularly worrisome, given the effects we've seen and the feeling that we haven't seen even the tip of the iceberg. For example, a recent study by the US Department of Justice estimated that between 2013 and 2018 nine Iranians working for the Islamic Revolutionary Guard stole 31.5 terabytes of documents and data from almost 8,000 professors at 320 universities around the world. Almost 4,000 of the professors were Americans, and the report estimated that it cost the 144 US universities that employed them some $3.4 billion dollars in lost data. Stolen data are one thing, but the significance begins to pale in comparison to what hackers can do to provoke social unrest and violence, especially when we leave doors wide open for them. What happened at the University of Missouri in terms of producing fear among students, particularly black students, came about in large part because of bad decisions that were made well beforehand, which created a golden opportunity for Russian hackers to act in provocative ways. The fact that they could, in a matter of hours, use a small number of users and approximately seventy bots to hijack Twitter trends and create scenarios in which the KKK and other extremist organizations were running rampant through the streets of Columbia in search of blacks to beat up should cause considerable concern. Of even more concern should be the chilling fact that the bots successfully evaded the algorithms Twitter used to protect against bot tweeting. As Orson Welles proved with his 1938 broadcast of H. G.

Wells's *The War of the Worlds*, it doesn't take a military invasion to create shock and awe. "Live" reports of a Martian invasion worked just fine. Today, a few hackers who understand how people with access to social media behave when confronted with incredible "news" will do just as well. If we are no better about where we get our information than that, then we can be assured that most of our decisions will be suboptimal, if not downright deadly.

If we turn into creatures of the southeast, we might as well crowd-source all of our decisions. Why worry about the underlying causes of global warming when we can see what tens of millions of our closest friends think? Why worry about Russian hackers working to rig an election when we can simply turn to some politicians and find out that it's "FAKE NEWS!!"? That way, we can rest easy because decisions have been made for us, and we can return to the serious business of chatting on Facebook with people whom we've never met. Or we can follow a conspiracy theory that the Sandy Hook Elementary School massacre in Newtown, Connecticut, in 2012 was a hoax perpetrated by the American government. And if we spend lots of time on Facebook, we might find it plausible that the platform was built to eat up as much of our time and conscious attention as possible. And while we're at it, we don't have to answer that "fake" jury summons we got in the mail today because verdicts are now being crowdsourced. Don't worry, though. You can still get all the chills and thrills of the courtroom because trials will be televised, especially those with the highest pretrial Nielsen rating. Move over, Judge Judy, because your cheating-roommate story is small potatoes compared to a juicy murder trial. By the way, make sure you check the Harrah's odds and lay down some pretrial bets on what the crowdsourced verdict will be.

Speaking of Harrah's, also make sure you check the over and under for the Sunday night game between the Patriots and the Saints. Now that the games are played electronically, with action figures so realistic they've put Madden NFL Football out of business, you don't have to worry that between Tuesday and Sunday Brady will pull up with a leg injury. You'll still have to worry about the "random" events—fumbles, interceptions, and the like—that the computer throws in to keep things interesting, but the NFL has created a rule that players are never injured. This will be great news to the millions of us with Fantasy Football teams. Plus, the players can last forever, or until they're crowdsourced out, at which point they're retired. Life is certainly different in the southeast.

BIBLIOGRAPHY

Preface

Anolik, Lili. "How O. J. Simpson Killed Popular Culture." *Vanity Fair*, May 7, 2014.

Bentley, Alex, Mark Earls, and Michael J. O'Brien. *I'll Have What She's Having: Mapping Social Behavior*. Cambridge, MA: MIT Press, 2011.

Bentley, R. Alexander, and Michael J. O'Brien. *The Acceleration of Cultural Change: From Ancestors to Algorithms*. Cambridge, MA: MIT Press, 2017.

Bentley, R. Alexander, Michael J. O'Brien, and William A. Brock. "Mapping Collective Behavior in the Big-Data Era." *Behavioral and Brain Sciences* 37 (2014): 63–119.

Kahneman, Daniel. *Thinking Fast and Slow*. New York: Farrar, Straus and Giroux, 2013.

Lewis, Michael. *The Undoing Project: A Friendship That Changed Our Minds*. New York: Norton, 2016.

Newton, Jim, and Shawn Hubler. "Simpson Held after Wild Chase: He's Charged with Murder of Ex-Wife, Friend." *Los Angeles Times*, June 18, 1994. http://www.latimes.com/local/la-oj-anniv-arrest-story.html.

Prechter, Robert R., ed. *Socionomic Studies of Society and Culture: How Social Mood Shapes Trends from Film to Fashion.* Gainesville, GA: Socionomics Institute Press, 2017.

Thaler, Richard H. *Misbehaving: The Making of Behavioral Economics.* New York: Norton, 2016.

Chapter 1

Alland, Alexander, Jr. "Cultural Evolution: The Darwinian Model." *Social Biology* 19 (1972): 227–239.

Bentley, R. Alexander, and Michael J. O'Brien. "The Selectivity of Social Learning and the Tempo of Cultural Evolution." *Journal of Evolutionary Psychology* 9 (2011): 125–141.

Bettinger, Robert L., and Peter J. Richerson. "The State of Evolutionary Archaeology: Evolutionary Correctness, or the Search for the Common Ground." In *Darwinian Archaeologies,* edited by Herbert D. G. Maschner, 221–231. New York: Plenum, 1996.

Binford, Lewis R. "Post-Pleistocene Adaptations." In *New Perspectives in Archeology,* edited by Sally R. Binford and Lewis R. Binford, 21–49. Chicago: Aldine, 1968.

Braidwood, Robert J. "Archeology and the Evolutionary Theory." In *Evolution and Anthropology: A Centennial Appraisal,* edited by B. J. Meggers, 76–89. Washington, DC: Anthropological Society of Washington, 1959.

Braidwood, Robert J., and Charles A. Reed. "The Achievement and Early Consequences of Food Production." *Cold Spring Harbor Symposia on Quantitative Biology* 22 (1957): 19–31.

Childe, V. Gordon. "The Urban Revolution." *Town Planning Review* 21 (1950): 3–17.

Flannery, Kent V. "A Visit to the Master." In *Guilá Naquitz: Archaic Foraging and Early Agriculture in Oaxaca, Mexico*, edited by K. V. Flannery, 511–519. Orlando, FL: Academic Press, 1986.

Hole, Frank, Kent V. Flannery, and James A. Neely. *Prehistory and Human Ecology of the Deh Luran Plain: An Early Village Sequence from Khuzistan, Iran*. Memoir, no. 1, Museum of Anthropology, University of Michigan. Ann Arbor, 1969.

Lathrap, Donald. "Review of *The Origins of Agriculture: An Evolutionary Perspective*, by David Rindos." *Economic Geography* 60 (1984): 339–344.

Leacock, Eleanor. "Introduction to Part I." In *Ancient Society* (1877), by Lewis Henry Morgan, i–xx. New York: Meridian, 1963.

Los Angeles Times. "The O.J. Simpson Murder Trial, by the Numbers," April 5, 2016. http://www.latimes.com/entertainment/la-et-archives-oj -simpson-trial-by-the-numbers-20160405-snap-htmlstory.html.

Mesoudi, Alex. "An Experimental Simulation of the 'Copy-Successful-Individuals' Cultural Learning Strategy: Adaptive Landscapes, Producer–Scrounger Dynamics, and Informational Access Costs." *Evolution and Human Behavior* 29 (2008): 350–363.

Morgan, Lewis Henry. *Ancient Society*. New York: Holt, 1877.

Muthukrishna, Michael, and Joseph Henrich. "Innovation in the Collective Brain." *Philosophical Transactions of the Royal Society B* 371 (2016): 20150192.

Rindos, David. *The Origins of Agriculture: An Evolutionary Perspective*. Orlando, FL: Academic Press, 1984.

Scott, James C. *Against the Grain: A Deep History of the Earliest States*. New Haven, CT: Yale University Press, 2017.

Shennan, Stephen J., and J. R. Wilkinson. "Ceramic Style Change and Neutral Evolution: A Case Study from Neolithic Europe." *American Antiquity* 66 (2001): 577–594.

Surowiecki, James. *The Wisdom of Crowds: Why the Many Are Smarter Than the Few.* London: Abacus, 2004.

Tylor, Edward B. *Primitive Culture.* London: Murray, 1871.

Chapter 2

Darwin, Charles. *On the Origin of Species by Means of Natural Selection, or the Preservation of Favoured Races in the Struggle for Life.* London: Murray, 1859.

Endler, John A. *Natural Selection in the Wild.* Princeton, NJ: Princeton University Press, 1986.

Lamarck, Jean-Baptiste. *Philosophie Zoologique, ou Exposition des Considérations Relatives à l'Histoire Naturelle des Animaux.* Paris: Museum d'Histoire Naturelle, 1809.

Leonard, Robert D. "Evolutionary Archaeology." In *Archaeological Theory Today*, edited by Ian Hodder, 65–97. Cambridge: Polity Press, 2001.

Mill, John Stuart. "On the Definition of Political Economy, and on the Method of Investigation Proper to It." *London and Westminster Review*, October 1836.

Nelson, Philip. "Information and Consumer Behavior." *Journal of Political Economy* 78 (1970): 311–329.

Smith, Adam. *An Inquiry into the Nature and Causes of the Wealth of Nations.* London: Strahan and Cadell, 1776.

Chapter 3

Bergstrom, Theodore C. "Evolution of Social Behavior: Individual and Group Selection." *Journal of Economic Perspectives* 16 (2002): 67–88.

Bilalić, Merim. *The Neuroscience of Expertise.* Cambridge: Cambridge University Press, 2017.

Brown, Mark. "How Driving a Taxi Changes London Cabbies' Brains." *Wired*, September 12, 2011.

Dennett, Daniel C. *Darwin's Dangerous Idea*. New York: Simon & Schuster, 1995.

Drachman, David A. "Do We Have Brain to Spare?" *Neurology* 64 (2005): 2004–2005.

Duch, Jordi, Joshua S. Waitzman, and Luís A. N. Amaral. "Quantifying the Performance of Individual Players in a Team Activity." *PLOS ONE* 5(6) (2010): e10937.

Gaines, Cork. "How the Patriots Pulled Off the Biggest Steal in NFL Draft History and Landed Future Hall of Famer Tom Brady." *Business Insider*, September 10, 2015.

Gould, Stephen J. *Wonderful Life: The Burgess Shale and the Nature of History*. New York: Norton, 1989.

Lehrer, Jonah. *How We Decide*. Boston: Houghton Mifflin Harcourt, 2009.

Maguire, Eleanor A., Katherine Woollett, and Hugo J. Spiers. "London Taxi Drivers and Bus Drivers: A Structural MRI and Neuropsychological Analysis." *Hippocampus* 16 (2006): 1091–1101.

Massey, Cade, and Richard H. Thaler. "The Loser's Curse: Decision Making and Market Efficiency in the National Football League Draft." *Management Science* 59 (2013): 1479–1495.

Pinker, Steven. "The False Lure of Group Selection." *Wired*, June 18, 2012.

Siegel, Daniel J. *Mind: A Journey to the Heart of Being Human*. New York: Norton, 2016.

Sober, Elliott, and David Sloan Wilson. *Unto Others: The Evolution and Psychology of Unselfish Behavior*. Cambridge, MA: Harvard University Press, 1999.

Soltis, Joseph, Robert Boyd, and Peter Richerson. "Can Group-Functional Behaviors Evolve by Cultural Group Selection? An Empirical Test." *Current Anthropology* 36 (1995): 473–483.

Williams, George C. *Adaptation and Natural Selection: A Critique of Some Current Evolutionary Thought.* Princeton, NJ: Princeton University Press, 1966.

Wilson, David Sloan, and Edward O. Wilson. "Evolution 'for the Good of the Group.'" *American Scientist* 96 (2008): 380–389.

Woollett, Katherine, and Eleanor A. Maguire. "Acquiring the 'Knowledge' of London's Layout Drives Structural Brain Changes." *Current Biology* 21 (2011): 2109–2114.

Chapter 4

Bentley, R. Alexander, and Michael J. O'Brien. "The Selectivity of Cultural Learning and the Tempo of Cultural Evolution." *Journal of Evolutionary Psychology* 9 (2011): 125–141.

Bloom, Paul. "Can a Dog Learn a Word?" *Science* 304 (2004): 1605–1606.

Boyd, Robert. *A Different Kind of Animal: How Culture Transformed Our Species.* Princeton, NJ: Princeton University Press, 2017.

Boyd, Robert, and Peter J. Richerson. *Culture and the Evolutionary Process.* Chicago: University of Chicago Press, 1985.

Caldwell, Christine A., and Alisa E. Millen. "Social Learning Mechanisms and Cumulative Culture: Is Imitation Necessary?" *Psychological Science* 12 (2009): 1478–1483.

Fragaszy, Dorothy M. "Community Resources for Learning: How Capuchin Monkeys Construct Technical Traditions." *Biological Theory* 6 (2011): 231–240.

Fridland, Ellen, and Richard Moore. "Imitation Reconsidered." *Philosophical Psychology* 28 (2015): 856–880.

Grassmann, Susanne, Juliane Kaminski, and Michael Tomasello. "How Two Word-Trained Dogs Integrate Pointing and Naming." *Animal Cognition* 15 (2012): 657–665.

Henrich, Joseph, and Francisco Gil-White. "The Evolution of Prestige: Freely Conferred Deference as a Mechanism for Enhancing the Benefits of Cultural Transmission." *Evolution and Human Behavior* 22 (2001): 165–196.

Heyes, Cecilia M., and Bennett G. Galef, Jr., eds. *Learning in Animals: The Roots of Culture*. San Diego: Academic Press, 1996.

Hirata, Satoshi, Kunio Watanabe, and Masao Kawai. "'Sweet-Potato Washing' Revisited." In *Primate Origins of Human Cognition and Behavior*, edited by Tetsuro Matsuzawa, 487–508. Tokyo: Springer, 2001.

Kaminski, Juliane, Josep Call, and Julia Fischer. "Word Learning in a Domestic Dog: Evidence for 'Fast Mapping.'" *Science* 304 (2004): 1682–1683.

Laland, Kevin N. "Social Learning Strategies." *Learning & Behavior* 32 (2004): 4–14.

Lehrer, Jonah. *How We Decide*. Boston: Houghton Mifflin Harcourt, 2009.

Mesoudi, Alex. "An Experimental Simulation of the 'Copy-Successful-Individuals' Cultural Learning Strategy: Adaptive Landscapes, Producer–Scrounger Dynamics, and Informational Access Costs." *Evolution and Human Behavior* 29 (2008): 350–363.

Mesoudi, Alex. "Variable Acquisition Costs Constrain Cumulative Cultural Evolution." *PLOS ONE* 6(3) (2011): e18239.

Morin, Roc. "A Conversation with Koko the Gorilla." *The Atlantic*, August 28, 2015. https://www.theatlantic.com/technology/archive/2015/08/koko -the-talking-gorilla-sign-language-francine-patterson/402307.

O'Brien, Michael J., Matthew T. Boulanger, Briggs Buchanan, Mark Collard, R. Lee Lyman, and John Darwent. "Innovation and Cultural Transmission in the American Paleolithic: Phylogenetic Analysis of Eastern Paleoindian Projectile-Point Classes." *Journal of Anthropological Archaeology* 34 (2014): 100–119.

O'Brien, Michael J., and Briggs Buchanan. "Cultural Learning and the Clovis Colonization of North America." *Evolutionary Anthropology* 26 (2017): 270–284.

Pilley, John W., and Hilary Hinzmann. *Chaser: Unlocking the Genius of the Dog Who Knows a Thousand Words.* New York: Houghton Mifflin Harcourt, 2013.

Preston, Douglas D. "Woody's Dream." *New Yorker* 75 (1999): 80–87.

Sholts, Sabrina B., Dennis J. Stanford, Louise M. Flores, and Sebastian K. T. S. Wärmländer. "Flake Scar Patterns of Clovis Points Analyzed with a New Digital Morphometrics Approach: Evidence for Direct Transmission of Technological Knowledge across Early North America." *Journal of Archaeological Science* 39 (2012): 3018–3026.

Tomasello, Michael, Malinda Carpenter, Josep Call, Tanya Behne, and Henricke Moll. "Understanding and Sharing Intentions: The Origins of Cultural Cognition." *Behavioral and Brain Sciences* 28 (2005): 675–735.

Tomasello, Michael, Ann C. Kruger, and Hilary H. Ratner. "Cultural Learning." *Behavioral and Brain Sciences* 16 (1993): 495–552.

Wells, H. G. *The Time Machine.* London, Heinemann, 1895.

Whiten, Andrew, Jane Goodall, William C. McGrew, Tsukasa Nishida, David V. Reynolds, Yukihiko Sugiyama, Caroline E. G. Tutin, et al. "Cultures in Chimpanzees." *Nature* 399 (1999): 682–685.

Whiten, Andrew, Nicola McGuigan, Sarah Marshall-Pescini, and Lydia M. Hopper. "Emulation, Imitation, Over-imitation and the Scope of Culture for Child and Chimpanzee." *Philosophical Transactions of the Royal Society B* 364 (2009): 2417–2428.

Chapter 5

Carroll, Lewis. *Through the Looking Glass and What Alice Found There.* London: Macmillan, 1872.

Complexity Labs. "Fitness Landscapes." February 15, 2014. http://complexitylabs.io/fitness-landscapes.

Kameda, Tatsuya, and Daisuke Nakanishi. "Cost-Benefit Analysis of Social/Cultural Learning in a Nonstationary Uncertain Environment: An Evolutionary Simulation and an Experiment with Human Subjects." *Evolution and Human Behavior* 23 (2002): 373–393.

Kane, David. "Local Hillclimbing on an Economic Landscape." Santa Fe Institute Working Paper 96-08-065, Santa Fe, NM, 1996.

Kang, Cecilia. "Unemployed Detroit Residents Are Trapped by a Digital Divide." *New York Times*, May 22, 2016. https://www.nytimes.com/2016/05/23/technology/unemployed-detroit-residents-are-trapped-by-a-digital-divide.html.

Kauffman, Stuart. *At Home in the Universe: The Search for Laws of Self-Organization and Complexity.* Oxford: Oxford University Press, 1995.

Kauffman, Stuart, José Lobo, and William J. Macready. "Optimal Search on a Technology Landscape." *Journal of Economic Behavior and Organization* 43 (2000): 141–166.

Kempe, Marius, Stephen J. Lycett, and Alex Mesoudi. "An Experimental Test of the Accumulated Copying Error Model of Cultural Mutation for Acheulean Handaxe Size." *PLOS ONE* 7(11) (2012): e48333.

National Student Clearinghouse Research Center. "Current Term Enrollment Estimates—Spring 2017." https://nscresearchcenter.org/currenttermenrollmentestimate-spring2017.

Page, Scott E. *Diversity and Complexity.* Princeton, NJ: Princeton University Press, 2011.

Simon, Caroline. "For-Profit Colleges' Teachable Moment: 'Terrible Outcomes Are Very Profitable." *Forbes*, March 19, 2018. https://www.forbes.com/sites/schoolboard/2018/03/19/for-profit-colleges-teachable-moment-terrible-outcomes-are-very-profitable/#3d7b01a440f5.

Tomasello, Michael, Ann C. Kruger, and Hilary H. Ratner. "Cultural Learning." *Behavioral and Brain Sciences* 16 (1993): 495–511.

Vaughan, C. David. "A Million Years of Style and Function: Regional and Temporal Variation in Acheulean Handaxes." In *Style and Function: Conceptual Issues in Evolutionary Archaeology*, edited by Teresa D. Hurt and Gordon F. M. Rakita, 141–163. Westport, CT: Bergin & Garvey.

Wright, Sewall. "The Roles of Mutation, Inbreeding, Crossbreeding and Selection in Evolution." In *Proceedings of the Sixth Congress on Genetics* (vol. 1), edited by Donald F. Jones, 356–366. New York: Brooklyn Botanic Garden, 1932.

Chapter 6

Atkisson, Curtis, Michael J. O'Brien, and Alex Mesoudi. "Adult Learners in a Novel Environment Use Prestige-Biased Social Learning." *Evolutionary Psychology* 10 (2012): 519–537.

Bentley, Alex, Mark Earls, and Michael J. O'Brien. *I'll Have What She's Having: Mapping Social Behavior.* Cambridge, MA: MIT Press, 2011.

Bentley, R. Alexander, Mark Earls, and Michael J. O'Brien. "Mapping Human Behavior for Business." *European Business Review* May–June (2012): 23–26.

Bentley, R. Alexander, Michael J. O'Brien, and William A. Brock. "Mapping Collective Behavior in the Big-Data Era." *Behavioral and Brain Sciences* 37 (2014): 63–119.

Brock, William A., R. Alexander Bentley, Michael J. O'Brien, and Camila S. S. Caiado. "Estimating a Path through a Map of Decision Making." *PLOS ONE* 9 (11) (2014): e111022.

Brock, William A., and Steven N. Durlauf. "Discrete Choice with Social Interactions." *Review of Economic Studies* 68 (2001): 235–260.

Ehrenberg, Andrew S. C. "The Pattern of Consumer Purchases." *Journal of the Royal Statistical Society C* 8 (1959): 26–41.

Enquist, Magnus, Kimmo Eriksson, and Stefano Ghirlanda. "Critical Social Learning: A Solution to Rogers's Paradox of Nonadaptive Culture." *American Anthropologist* 109 (2007): 727–734.

Kahneman, Daniel. "Maps of Bounded Rationality: Psychology for Behavioral Economics." *American Economic Review* 93 (2003): 1449–1475.

Laland, Kevin N. "Social Learning Strategies." *Learning & Behavior* 32 (2004): 4–14.

Loewenstein, George F., Leigh Thompson, and Max Bazerman. "Social Utility and Decision Making in Interpersonal Contexts." *Journal of Personality and Social Psychology* 57 (1989): 426–441.

Mesoudi, Alex. "An Experimental Simulation of the 'Copy-Successful-Individuals' Cultural Learning Strategy: Adaptive Landscapes, Producer–Scrounger Dynamics, and Informational Access Costs." *Evolution and Human Behavior* 29 (2008): 350–363.

Mesoudi, Alex, and Stephen J. Lycett. "Random Copying, Frequency-Dependent Copying and Culture Change." *Evolution and Human Behavior* 30 (2009): 41–48.

Pariser, Eli. *The Filter Bubble: What the Internet Is Hiding from You*. New York: Penguin, 2011.

Rogers, Everett M. *Diffusion of Innovations*, 4th ed. New York: Free Press, 1995.

Salganik, Matthew J., Peter S. Dodds, and Duncan J. Watts. "Experimental Study of Inequality and Unpredictability in an Artificial Cultural Market." *Science* 311 (2006): 854–856.

Chapter 7

Anonymous. "Playing Out the Last Hand." *The Economist*, April 26, 2014. https://www.economist.com/news/briefing/21601240-warren-buffetts-50-years-running-berkshire-hathaway-have-been-one-businesss-most-impressive.

Frazzini, Andrea, David Kabiller, and Lasse H. Pedersen. "Buffett's Alpha." National Bureau of Economic Research Working Paper No. 19681, 2013.

Keller, Rudi. "University of Missouri Enrollment to Decline More than 7 Percent; 400 Jobs to Be Eliminated." *Columbia Daily Tribune*, May 15, 2017.

Muggeridge, Malcolm. *Muggeridge through the Microphone: BBC Radio and Television*. London: British Broadcasting Corporation, 1967.

Prier, Jared. "Commanding the Trend: Social Media as Information Warfare." *Strategic Studies Quarterly* (Winter 2017): 50–85.

Richards, Jeffrey. *Sir Henry Irving: A Victorian Actor and His World*. London: Bloomsbury, 2005.

Schroeder, Alice. *The Snowball: Warren Buffett and the Business of Life*. New York: Bantam, 2008.

Stripling, Jack. "How Missouri's Deans Plotted to Get Rid of Their Chancellor." *Chronicle of Higher Education*, November 20, 2015.

Chapter 8

Acerbi, Alberto, Vasileios Lampos, Philip Garnett, and R. Alexander Bentley. "The Expression of Emotion in 20th Century Books." *PLOS ONE* 8(3) (2013): e59030.

Allen, David, and T. D. Wilson. Information Overload: Context and Causes. *New Review of Information Behaviour Research* 4 (2003): 31–44.

Andris, Clio, David Lee, Marcus J. Hamilton, Mauro Martino, Christian E. Gunning, and John Armistead Selden. "The Rise of Partisanship and Super-Cooperators in the U.S. House of Representatives." *PLOS ONE* 10(4) (2015): e0123507.

Beinhocker, Eric D. *The Origin of Wealth: Evolution, Complexity, and the Radical Remaking of Economics.* New York: Random House, 2006.

Bentley, Alex, Mark Earls, and Michael J. O'Brien. *I'll Have What She's Having: Mapping Social Behavior.* Cambridge, MA: MIT Press, 2011.

Bentley, R. Alexander, and Michael J. O'Brien. *The Acceleration of Cultural Change: From Ancestors to Algorithms.* Cambridge, MA: MIT Press, 2017.

Borgatti, Stephen P., Ajay Mehra, Daniel J. Brass, and Giuseppe Labianca. "Network Analysis in the Social Sciences." *Science* 323 (2009): 892–895.

Brock, William A., and Steven N. Durlauf. "A Formal Model of Theory Choice in Science." *Economic Theory* 14 (1999): 113–130.

Cohen, Jon. "U.S. Blames 'Massive' Hack of Research Data on Iran." *Science* 359 (2018): 1450.

Evans, James A., and Jacob G. Foster. "Metaknowledge." *Science* 331 (2011): 721–725.

Garimella, Kiran, and Ingmar Weber. "A Long-Term Analysis of Polarization on Twitter." *arXiv* (2017): 1703.02769.

Henrich, Joseph, and James Broesch. "On the Nature of Cultural Transmission Networks: Evidence from Fijian Villages for Adaptive Learning Biases." *Philosophical Transactions of the Royal Society B* 366 (2011): 1139–1148.

Iyengar, Sheena S., and Mark R. Lepper. "When Choice Is Demotivating: Can One Desire Too Much of a Good Thing?" *Journal of Personality and Social Psychology* 79 (2000): 995–1006.

Jacoby, Jacob, Donald E. Speller, and Carol A. Kohn. "Brand Choice Behavior as a Function of Information Load." *Journal of Marketing Research* 11 (1974): 63–69.

Jinha, Arif. "Article 50 Million: An Estimate of the Number of Scholarly Articles in Existence." *Learned Publishing* 23 (2010): 258–263.

Kahneman, Daniel. "Maps of Bounded Rationality: Psychology for Behavioral Economics." *American Economic Review* 93 (2003): 1449–1475.

Kim, Tae. "John Malone Says Amazon Is a Death Star Moving within 'Striking Range' of Every Industry on the Planet." November 16, 2017. https://www.msn.com/en-us/money/companies/john-malone-says -amazon-is-a-death-star-moving-in-striking-range-of-every-industry-on -the-planet/ar-BBF2LYS?li=BBnbfcL.

Kircher, Madison M. "Sean Parker: We Built Facebook to Exploit You." November 9, 2017. https://www.msn.com/en-us/news/technology/sean -parker-we-built-facebook-to-exploit-you/ar-BBELRgF?li=BBnb7Kz.

Kitcher, Philip. *Abusing Science: The Case against Creationism*. Cambridge, MA: MIT Press, 1982.

Lazer, David M. J., Matthew A. Baum, Yochai Benkler, Adam J. Berinski, Kelly M. Greenhill, Filippo Menczer, Miriam J. Metzger, et al. "The Science of Fake News: Addressing Fake News Requires a Multidisciplinary Effort." *Science* 359 (2018): 1094–1096.

Onnela, Jukka-Pekka, and Felix Reed-Tsochas. "Spontaneous Emergence of Social Influence in Online Systems." *Proceedings of the National Academy of Sciences* 107 (2010): 18375–18380.

Prier, Jared. "Commanding the Trend: Social Media as Information Warfare." *Strategic Studies Quarterly* (Winter 2017): 50–85.

Salganik, Matthew J., Peter S. Dodds, and Duncan J. Watts. "Experimental Study of Inequality and Unpredictability in an Artificial Cultural Market." *Science* 311 (2006): 854–856.

Schrift, Rom Y., Oded Netzer, and Ran Kivetz. "Complicating Choice: The Effort Compatibility Hypothesis." *Journal of Marketing Research* 48 (2011): 308–326.

Sela, Aner, and Jonah Berger. "Decision Quicksand: How Trivial Choices Suck Us In." *Journal of Consumer Research* 39 (2012): 360–370.

Vosoughi, Soroush, Deb Roy, and Sinan Aral. "The Spread of True and False News Online." *Science* 359 (2018): 1146–1151.

Ware, Mark, and Michael Mabe. *The STM Report: An Overview of Scientific and Scholarly Journal Publishing.* Oxford: International Association of Scientific, Technical and Medical Publishers, 2015.

Watts, Duncan, and Steve Hasker. "Marketing in an Unpredictable World." *Harvard Business Review* 84(9) (2006): 25–30.

INDEX

Voir dire, xiv